AI FOR SEO ESSENTIALS

A COMPREHENSIVE GUIDE TO LEVERAGING ARTIFICIAL INTELLIGENCE FOR ENHANCED SEARCH ENGINE OPTIMIZATION, CONTENT CREATION, AND DIGITAL MARKETING SUCCESS

ANDREW BUS

REX PUBLISHING

INTRODUCTION

Welcome to the fascinating world of AI and SEO! In this book, we're going to explore how artificial intelligence is revolutionizing the landscape of search engine optimization. Don't worry if these terms sound intimidating - we'll break everything down into easy-to-understand concepts that anyone can grasp, regardless of their technical background.

Imagine you have a website, and you want more people to find it when they search online. That's what SEO, or Search Engine Optimization, is all about. It's the art and science of making your website more visible and attractive to search engines like Google. Now, AI, or Artificial Intelligence, is like a super-smart helper that can make this process easier, faster, and more effective than ever before.

In this book, we'll start by explaining what AI is and how it works in simple, everyday terms. You'll learn about the different types of AI and how they're being used in various industries. Then, we'll dive into the exciting ways AI is being applied to create content for websites and how this is reshaping the world of SEO.

We'll explore a range of tools available to you, from basic text generators that can help you write articles, to more complex systems that can automate entire processes like content creation, image generation, and even social media posting. You'll discover how these tools can save you time and boost your online presence.

One of the most crucial aspects we'll cover is Google's stance on AI-created content. As the biggest search engine, Google's opinion can make or break your website's success. We'll break down what Google has officially said about AI content and what it means for your SEO strategy.

Throughout the book, we'll share real-world examples and case studies of businesses and individuals who have successfully leveraged AI in their SEO efforts. You'll see how AI can be applied in different industries and for various purposes, from e-commerce to blogging and beyond.

We'll also address some of the challenges and potential pitfalls of using AI for SEO. You'll learn about the ethical considerations, the importance of maintaining quality and originality, and how to strike the right balance between AI assistance and human creativity.

Whether you're a small business owner looking to improve your online visibility, a content creator wanting to streamline your process, or simply someone curious about the future of digital marketing, this book has something valuable for you. We'll provide practical tips and strategies that you can start implementing right away, even if you're not a tech expert.

So, get ready to embark on an exciting journey into the world of AI-powered SEO. We'll demystify complex concepts, provide you with actionable insights, and help you unlock the immense potential of AI in boosting your online presence. By the end of this book, you'll have a clear understanding of how AI is shaping the future of SEO and how you can harness its power to stay ahead in the digital world.

Let's dive in and discover together how AI is transforming the way we approach SEO, and how you can use these cutting-edge technologies to your advantage in the ever-evolving digital landscape.

1

WHAT IS GENERATIVE AI?

“Artificial intelligence is the new electricity.”
- **Andrew Ng**

This chapter introduces the concept of Generative AI, an advanced type of artificial intelligence that can create new content such as text, images, music, and videos based on patterns in provided data. Unlike traditional AI, which primarily analyzes and processes data, generative AI can produce entirely new and unique outputs.

Key points covered include:

- Content Creation: Generative AI’s ability to create various forms of art and media, like articles, poetry, and music.

- Learning from Data: How generative AI uses large datasets to recognize patterns and generate new, similar content.
- Practical Applications: The diverse use cases of generative AI in fields such as marketing, medicine, graphic design, and more.

The chapter also delves into the history of generative AI, from early neural networks in the 1950s to the introduction of significant models like GANs in the 2010s. It explains important algorithms and techniques, including Generative Adversarial Networks (GANs), Variational Autoencoders (VAEs), Transformer Models, and Deep Convolutional Networks (DCNs).

ADDITIONALLY, practical applications in art, medicine, marketing, games, and natural language processing are discussed. The chapter concludes by addressing the challenges and future of generative AI, touching on ethics, copyright issues, and its potential to revolutionize various industries.

GENERATIVE AI IS a type of artificial intelligence that can create new content based on provided data and patterns. Unlike traditional AI, which primarily analyzes and processes data, generative AI can produce something entirely new from the given information.

Here are some key aspects of generative AI:

1. Content Creation: Generative AI can create text, images, music, and other forms of art. For example, language models like GPT-4 can write articles, compose poetry, or engage in conversations.
2. Learning from Data: Generative AI is trained on vast datasets, enabling it to recognize patterns and structures within the data. This allows it to generate new, similar content.
3. Practical Applications: Generative AI is used in various fields such as marketing content creation, automatic code generation, graphic design, music composition, and even in medicine, where it can assist in developing new drugs.

Generative AI is capable of a wide range of creative tasks across different mediums. For text creation, tools like OpenAI's GPT-4 and Claude Sonet excel at writing articles, stories, or poems, showcasing their versatility in language processing. In the realm of image creation, technologies such as DALL-E, MidJourney, StableDiffusion, and Leonardo are transforming how pictures and graphics are produced, allowing for unprecedented levels of artistic expression. Music creation is another area where AI shines, with platforms like Suno, Udio, MusicGen, Stable Audio, MusicLM, and Riffusion enabling the composition of music tracks that cater to varied tastes and genres. Additionally, video creation technologies like Sora, Runway, and Motion Diffusion are making it possible to produce short films or animations, demonstrating the expansive capabilities of AI in media production. These tools collectively illustrate the transformative impact of generative AI across multiple creative domains.

GENERATIVE AI DIFFERS from traditional AI systems in that it doesn't just analyze and classify data but actively creates new, unique content based on the knowledge it has acquired.

1.1 The History of Generative AI

Generative AI is a type of technology that can create new things; just like humans can. It might be text, images, sounds, or even videos. It's a bit like having a very smart robot that can paint, write stories, or compose music!

1.1.1. The Early Years

The story of generative AI began a long time ago, in the 1950s and 1960s. It was like we were learning to build the first blocks that would later become a big castle.

In those days, scientists started creating the first "computer brains," which we call neural networks. Imagine these networks are like spider webs made of tiny computers that learn to solve problems together.

IN THE 1980S, more advanced models were created, like genetic algorithms. This was a bit like teaching computers to copy the way plants and animals evolve in nature.

1.1.2. The 90s and 2000s

During this time, scientists invented new ways for computers to learn better from data. It's like we gave computers big books full of information and taught them how to use them.

PROBABILISTIC MODELS WERE CREATED THEN, such as Hidden Markov Models. This sounds complicated, but imagine it's like a guessing game where the computer tries to predict what will happen next based on what it already knows.

NEURAL NETWORKS and unsupervised learning algorithms also developed during this time. It's a bit like letting computers learn on their own, without constantly telling them what to do.

1.1.3. The Last Decade

In 2014, something really breakthrough happened - Generative Adversarial Networks (GANs) were invented. Imagine we have two robots: one tries to create fake images, and the other tries to guess which images are real and which are fake. This way, both robots get better and better at their tasks.

MORE RECENTLY, transformer models like GPT-3 and DALL-E were created. These are like super intelligent machines that can write texts and create images almost as well as humans. They use huge amounts of data to learn how the world works and how we humans create different things.

All these inventions have led to today's artificial intelligence that can do amazing things - write stories, paint pictures, and even compose music. It's still not as good as real artists, but it's getting better every year!

This history shows us how generative AI has grown from simple ideas to powerful tools that can create all sorts of things. It's exciting to think about what it might be able to do in the future!

1.2. Key Algorithms and Techniques

In this chapter, we'll learn about the special "recipes" that make generative AI work. These recipes are called algorithms, and they're like the secret ingredients that make AI so smart and creative.

1.2.1. Generative Adversarial Networks (GANs)

Imagine you have two robot friends: one is an artist, and the other is an art critic. The artist robot tries to create paintings that look real, while the critic robot tries to spot which paintings are fake. As they keep practicing, both robots get better at their jobs. The artist learns to make more realistic paintings, and the critic becomes better at spotting fakes.

. . .

This is how GANs work. They have two parts that compete with each other, helping both to improve. It's like a fun game that makes the AI smarter and better at creating things that look real.

1.2.2. Variational Autoencoders (VAEs)

Think of VAEs like a magic box that can shrink things down and then make them big again. But it's not just shrinking - it's learning about the important parts of what it's shrinking.

For example, if you put pictures of cats into this magic box, it learns what makes a cat look like a cat. Then, it can create new pictures of cats that it has never seen before! It's like it understands the "idea" of a cat and can imagine new ones.

1.2.3. Transformer Models

Transformer models are like super smart readers. Imagine you have a friend who can read a whole library in a day and remember everything! That's kind of what transformer models do with information.

These models are really good at understanding language. They can write stories, answer questions, and even translate languages. It's like they've learned how words work together to make sentences and stories.

One famous transformer model is called GPT (which stands for Generative Pre-trained Transformer). It's so good at writing that sometimes it's hard to tell if a human or the AI wrote something!

1.2.4. Deep Convolutional Networks (DCNs)

DCNs are like the eyes of AI. They're really good at looking at pictures and understanding what's in them. Imagine you could look at a thousand pictures in a second and remember every detail - that's what DCNs can do!

THESE NETWORKS ARE great for creating and changing images. They can take a picture of a dog and turn it into a painting, or they can create a completely new picture of a dog that doesn't exist in real life.

ALL THESE ALGORITHMS work together to make generative AI so powerful. They help AI understand and create text, images, music, and even videos. It's like giving a computer a paintbrush, a pen, and a musical instrument all at once!

BY LEARNING ABOUT THESE ALGORITHMS, we can understand how AI is able to be so creative. It's not magic - it's clever math and lots of practice with huge amounts of information. And who knows? Maybe one day you'll help create the next big algorithm that makes AI even smarter!

1.3 Practical Applications of Generative AI

Generative AI isn't just something scientists talk about in

labs. It's being used in many exciting ways in the real world. Let's explore some of these applications!

1.3.1 Art and Entertainment:

Generative AI is like a super creative artist that never gets tired. It can:

- Create amazing pictures: Imagine telling a computer "Draw a cat riding a unicycle on Mars," and it makes that picture for you!
- Make music: AI can compose new songs in different styles. It's like having a musician who knows every instrument and can play any type of music.
- Help make movies: Some movies use AI to create special effects or even to help write scripts.

For example, there's an AI called DALL-E that can draw anything you describe to it. People have used it to create funny, beautiful, and sometimes weird art that no one has ever seen before!

1.3.2 Medicine

AI is becoming a helpful assistant to doctors. It can:

- Create fake patient data: This helps doctors practice without using real people's information.
- Design new medicines: AI can suggest new combinations of chemicals that might make good medicines.

- Read X-rays and scans: Sometimes AI can spot things in medical images that even doctors might miss.

For instance, there's an AI that helped design a new antibiotic to fight bacteria that other medicines couldn't beat. It's like having a super-smart scientist working non-stop to help keep people healthy!

1.3.3 Marketing and Advertising

AI is changing how companies tell people about their products:

- Writing ads: AI can write many different versions of an ad to see which one people like best.
- Creating images for ads: Just like with art, AI can make pictures for advertisements.
- Personalizing ads: AI can help show different ads to different people based on what they like.

A company called Phrasee uses AI to write email subject lines that make people want to open the emails. It's like having a friend who always knows the most interesting thing to say!

1.3.4 Games and Simulations

AI is making games more fun and helping people learn in new ways:

- Creating game worlds: AI can help make huge

game worlds filled with interesting things to explore.
- Making characters in games smarter: AI can make the characters in games act more like real people.
- Creating training simulations: These help people practice real jobs in a safe, computer-generated world.

For example, in a game called "No Man's Sky," AI creates entire planets for players to explore. Each planet is unique, with its own animals, plants, and landscapes. It's like having a magic machine that can create endless new worlds!

1.3.5 Natural Language Processing (NLP)

This is all about AI understanding and using human language:

- Chatbots: These are computer programs that can talk to people, answer questions, and help solve problems.
- Translation: AI can help translate languages, making it easier for people from different countries to understand each other.
- Summarizing text: AI can read long articles and write short summaries, like having a super-fast reader who can tell you the main points of any book in seconds.

A famous example is GPT-3, which can write stories, answer questions, and even help programmers write code.

It's like having a super-smart friend who knows a little bit about almost everything!

In all these areas, generative AI is helping people do things faster, create new and exciting things, and solve problems in ways we've never been able to before. It's an exciting time to learn about AI because new applications are being discovered all the time!

1.3.6 Sentiment Analysis

Generative AI is also really good at understanding how people feel about things. This is called sentiment analysis. It's like having a friend who can always tell if you're happy, sad, or angry just by listening to what you say!

Here are some ways generative AI helps with sentiment analysis:

- Understanding emotions in text: AI can read reviews, social media posts, or emails and figure out if the person writing is feeling positive, negative, or neutral. Imagine having a magic pair of glasses that could show you the emotions behind every text message!
- Helping businesses: Companies use this to understand what customers think about their products. It's like having a super-fast assistant who can read thousands of customer comments and tell you what most people like or don't like.

This helps companies make their products better.
- Improving customer service: AI can help identify upset customers quickly, so human helpers can step in to solve problems faster. It's like having a special alarm that rings when someone needs extra help.
- Analyzing social media trends: AI can look at millions of posts to see how people feel about current events or popular topics. It's like having a magic thermometer that can measure the mood of the whole internet!

For example, during big events like elections or sports tournaments, AI can analyze tweets to see how people are feeling. It's much faster than humans trying to read all those messages!

Some cool real-world uses of sentiment analysis include:

1. Movie studios using it to predict how well a new film will do based on early reviews.
2. Politicians using it to understand how people feel about different issues.
3. Hotels using it to quickly spot and respond to negative reviews.

Sentiment analysis shows how AI doesn't just understand the words we use, but can also pick up on the emotions behind them. This helps create better communication between people and machines, making our interactions with technology more natural and helpful.

. . .

It's exciting to think about how this technology might be used in the future. One day, we'll have AI assistants that can understand our moods and help cheer us up when we're feeling down!

1.4 Challenges and the Future

While generative AI is exciting and powerful, it also faces some big challenges. Let's explore these challenges and think about what the future might hold for this amazing technology.

1.4.1 Ethics and Copyright

One of the biggest questions about generative AI is: "Who owns what the AI creates?"

- Imagine an AI writes a beautiful song. Who should get credit for it? The person who made the AI, the company that owns it, or should the AI itself get credit?
- What if an AI creates a painting that looks very similar to a famous artist's work? Is that okay, or is it copying?

These are tricky questions that lawyers and lawmakers are trying to figure out. It's like when you play with your friends and create something together - sometimes it's hard to say who came up with which idea!

1.4.2 Understanding and Interpretation

Another challenge is that we don't always know how AI makes its decisions.

- It's like having a super-smart friend who always knows the answer, but can't explain how they figured it out.
- This can be a problem, especially in important areas like medicine or law, where we need to understand why decisions are made.

Scientists are working on making AI that can explain its thinking, kind of like a student showing their work in a math problem.

1.4.3 Bias and Fairness

AI learns from data, and sometimes that data can contain human biases.

- For example, if an AI learns from books written a long time ago, it might think old-fashioned ideas are still true today.
- This could lead to unfair treatment of certain groups of people.

It's important to make sure AI is fair to everyone, just like we try to be fair when we play games with our friends.

1.4.4 Job Changes

As AI gets better at doing things, some jobs might change or disappear.

- For instance, if AI can write news articles, what will happen to journalists?
- But AI might also create new jobs we haven't even thought of yet!

It's a bit like when computers were first invented - some jobs went away, but many new and exciting jobs were created too.

1.4.5 The Future of Generative AI

Despite these challenges, the future of generative AI looks very exciting!

- We might see AI that can create entire movies or video games based just on a story idea.
- AI could help solve big problems like climate change by coming up with new ideas that humans haven't thought of.
- In education, AI could create personalized lessons for each student, helping everyone learn in the way that's best for them.

Imagine having a super-smart, super-creative helper that can assist with almost anything. That's what generative AI might be like in the future!

1.4.6 Working Together

The most important thing to remember is that AI is a tool to help humans, not replace them.

- In the future, the best results will probably come from humans and AI working together.
- Humans can provide creativity, emotional understanding, and ethical judgment that AI might struggle with.

It's like having a super-powered paintbrush - it can help you create amazing art, but you're still the artist making the decisions!

As we move forward, it's important for everyone to learn about AI, understand its capabilities and limitations, and think about how we want to use this powerful technology. The future of generative AI is not just up to scientists and engineers - it's up to all of us to decide how we want to shape this exciting new world!

2

HUMAN-WRITTEN TEXT VS. AI

"The machine does not isolate man from the great problems of nature but plunges him more deeply into them."

- Antoine de Saint-Exupéry

This chapter explores the evolving landscape of text creation, highlighting the interplay between human input and artificial intelligence. In the modern digital age, texts are rarely crafted by humans alone; instead, they are a product of both human effort and machine assistance.

Key points covered include:

- Integration of AI in Writing: The chapter explains how AI tools, like Grammarly and other specialized solutions, have become essential in refining grammar, style, and overall quality of written content. This integration makes it challenging to distinguish between texts written solely by humans and those generated by AI.

- Role of Large Language Models (LLMs): It discusses how LLMs, trained on extensive datasets of human-written texts, generate content that closely mimics human writing, blurring the lines between human and machine authorship.
- Collaboration for Enhanced Productivity: AI tools are shown to assist writers by suggesting word choices, stylistic improvements, and even generating paragraphs, enhancing productivity and content quality across various fields, including marketing, academia, and technical writing.
- Predictive Text Generation: The chapter highlights the benefits of predictive text generation, which speeds up writing by anticipating the next word or sentence, thereby reducing the cognitive load on writers.
- Context-Aware Writing Assistants: AI's ability to analyze tone, sentiment, and intent is discussed, illustrating how it can fine-tune content for specific purposes, such as making marketing copy more persuasive or technical documents clearer.
- Challenges of Originality and Authenticity: The chapter raises important questions about the true authorship of AI-assisted content, emphasizing the need to balance AI's capabilities

with the preservation of human creativity and originality.
- Ethical Implications: It addresses the ethical concerns associated with AI-generated content, such as the potential for misuse and the importance of transparency and accountability to maintain trust in digital communication.

In conclusion, this chapter underscores the transformative impact of AI on text creation. While AI enhances efficiency and quality, it also challenges traditional notions of authorship and authenticity. As we embrace this new era, it is crucial to find a balance that leverages both human creativity and machine intelligence, fostering a collaborative future in digital writing.

~

In today's digital age, where texts are crafted on computers, tablets, or even phones, the concept of a document entirely written by a human no longer exists.

Even if the initial input is manually typed, all elements of the post-process have become an integral and indispensable part of the content creation workflow. Every text produced on a computer undergoes checks by algorithms that correct typos and punctuation errors.

Marketing agencies now employ a whole array of tools to enhance grammar and style. These range from well-known resources like Grammarly to less familiar or specialized AI-based solutions and large language models (LLMs).

As a result, it has become increasingly difficult to distinguish between texts written by humans and those generated by AI. Additionally, as I mentioned in the previous chapter, texts written by generative algorithms are based on vast amounts of data, including huge collections of texts ever written and digitized by humans. Such LLM systems typically generate what is most likely or similar to the texts they were trained on.

The data these models learn from are organic human texts. Therefore, an LLM that creates texts by mirroring the highest likelihood of resemblance to human-written texts sounds and appears as if it were written by a human.

This convergence of human and machine input in text creation has led to a new era in digital communication. The boundary between human creativity and machine efficiency is increasingly blurred. Writers and content creators are now collaborating with AI in ways that enhance productivity, accuracy, and creativity. AI tools can suggest word choices, provide stylistic recommendations, and even generate entire paragraphs based on the context provided by the human writer.

For instance, when drafting an article or an email, an AI tool might suggest alternative phrases that are more engaging or appropriate for the target audience. This not only saves time but also elevates the quality of the content. In academic writing, AI can help researchers by suggesting relevant sources, checking for plagiarism, and even formatting citations correctly. These tools have become essential in maintaining the high standards expected in professional and educational environments.

The integration of AI in writing extends beyond mere correction and suggestion. It includes predictive text generation, where the AI anticipates the next word or sentence a writer intends to type. This feature, widely used in smartphone keyboards and email applications, significantly speeds up the writing process and reduces cognitive load on the writer. As a result, writers can focus more on the creative and conceptual aspects of their work.

Furthermore, AI-powered writing assistants are becoming more context-aware. They can analyze the tone, sentiment, and intent of the text, providing suggestions to match the desired style. For example, a marketing copy intended to be persuasive and engaging can be fine-tuned to enhance its impact, while a technical document can be adjusted for clarity and precision. This level of sophistication ensures that the content is not only grammatically correct but also contextually appropriate and effective.

However, this reliance on AI also raises questions about originality and authenticity. If AI is contributing significantly to the creation of content, who is the true author?

This is particularly relevant in creative fields such as literature, journalism, and advertising, where the unique voice of the creator is highly valued. There is a growing need to balance the use of AI with the preservation of human creativity and originality.

Moreover, the ethical implications of AI-generated content cannot be ignored. The potential for misuse, such as generating deepfake text or manipulating information, poses significant challenges. Ensuring transparency and accountability in AI-assisted writing is crucial to maintaining trust and integrity in digital communication. As AI continues to evolve, it is essential to establish guidelines and standards that govern its use, ensuring that it complements rather than compromises human creativity.

In conclusion, the fusion of human and AI in text creation marks a transformative shift in how we write and communicate. While AI enhances efficiency and quality, it also challenges our notions of authorship and authenticity. As we navigate this new landscape, it is imperative to strike a balance that leverages the strengths of both human creativity and machine intelligence, fostering a collaborative future in digital writing.

3

CAN AI-WRITTEN TEXT BE RECOGNIZED?

"The question of whether a computer can think is no more interesting than the question of whether a submarine can swim."

- Edsger W. Dijkstra

In this intriguing chapter, we tackle a question that's on the minds of many SEO professionals and content creators: Is it possible to distinguish between text written by humans and text generated by AI?

We begin by exploring the current state of AI-generated content and how it has evolved to closely mimic human writing. You'll discover why this question has become increasingly relevant and challenging to answer as AI technology advances.

. . .

Throughout the chapter, we'll examine:

- The characteristics of AI-generated text and how they compare to human-written content
- The tools and techniques currently used to detect AI-written text
- The limitations and challenges of these detection methods
- Real-world examples and case studies of AI detection in action

We'll also delve into the implications of this blurring line between human and AI-generated content for SEO, content creation, and digital marketing as a whole. You'll gain insights into how search engines, readers, and content platforms are adapting to this new reality.

Additionally, we'll discuss the ethical considerations surrounding AI-generated content and the importance of transparency in its use. You'll learn about best practices for disclosing the use of AI in content creation and how this might affect user trust and engagement.

By the end of this chapter, you'll have a comprehensive understanding of the current landscape of AI text recognition. You'll be equipped with knowledge about the capabilities and limitations of AI detection tools, and how this impacts your content strategy.

Whether you're a content creator, marketer, or SEO professional, this chapter will provide you with valuable insights to navigate the complex world of AI-generated content and its detectability.

~

Having read everything I've written so far, you might already have some thoughts on this question.

Like any innovation, when a new method of production emerges, we seek ways to distinguish between items made using old and new techniques. For example, this was the case when the first synthetic diamonds appeared on the market. Initially, there were effective methods to differentiate between synthetic and natural diamonds. However, as the technology for producing diamonds improved, synthetic diamonds became indistinguishable from real ones.

This led to two phenomena: first, a significant drop in the price of natural diamonds. Second, in response to their inability to create any reliable method to tell whether a diamond was natural or synthetic, producers of natural diamonds simply introduced certifications.

. . .

THIS APPROACH MIGHT MAKE sense for luxury products or items that convey prestige. But what about everyday items? Here, certification indicating that something is made in a traditional manner is largely irrelevant.

THE SAME SITUATION applies or has applied to texts and content generated by AI. Initially, AI-generated content was relatively easy to identify, and many tools were developed for this purpose. OpenAI once released such a tool. However, as language models have been refined, prompts improved, and as people increasingly use auto-correction tools, style enhancers, and grammar editors like MS Word or Grammarly, it has become nearly impossible to distinguish AI-generated texts from human-written ones.

A TELLING example is when one of the most popular current tools for detecting AI-generated content was used to analyze a book of the Bible. The results were not only surprising but intriguing. As you might guess, the analysis suggested that the Bible was generated by AI.

WHY IS this finding so intriguing, and what does it tell us? It vividly illustrates a few points:

1. The basic principle of LLM models, as many explain in layman's terms, involves choosing the most likely next words based on probabilities. These probabilities are learned from vast amounts of text written by humans. Thus, a well-trained model can produce text that sets words in

a way that most likely resembles human writing. Therefore, there is no simple or reliable way to differentiate such text from that written by a human.

2. We've reached a stage where texts written by humans, or by humans with machine assistance, or even completely by machines using a good prompt and LLM, are indistinguishable.

So, this raises a critical question: If text written by a machine (an LLM model) is indistinguishable from text written by a human, what does this mean for internet search engines, for Google?

Does Google have its own methods for detecting AI-generated content?

Google itself has answered these questions. You can read about it in the next section.

4

GOOGLE'S STANCE ON AI-WRITTEN CONTENT

"The greatest danger in times of turbulence is not the turbulence; it is to act with yesterday's logic."

- Peter Drucker

In this pivotal chapter, we delve into one of the most crucial aspects of using AI for SEO: Google's official position on AI-generated content. As the dominant force in search, Google's stance significantly impacts how we approach AI in our SEO strategies.

We kick off by examining Google's official announcements regarding AI-written content. You'll gain a clear understanding of what the search giant considers acceptable and what it frowns upon. This information is vital for anyone looking to integrate AI into their content creation process without risking penalties or reduced visibility in search results.

NEXT, we break down Google's E-E-A-T guidelines (Experience, Expertise, Authoritativeness, and Trustworthiness) and how they apply to AI-generated content. You'll learn how to ensure your AI-created content aligns with these important quality markers that Google uses to evaluate web pages.

WE'LL ALSO EXPLORE:

- The evolution of Google's position on AI content over time
- How to strike a balance between AI efficiency and meeting Google's quality standards
- Practical tips for using AI in content creation while staying in Google's good graces

Throughout the chapter, we'll provide real-world examples and case studies that illustrate successful implementations of AI-generated content within Google's guidelines. These insights will help you navigate the sometimes tricky waters of AI and SEO.

BY THE END of this chapter, you'll have a comprehensive understanding of Google's perspective on AI-written content. This knowledge will empower you to make informed decisions about how to leverage AI in your SEO strategy while maintaining compliance with Google's guidelines and best practices.

Prepare to gain crucial insights that will shape your approach to AI in SEO and help you stay ahead in the ever-evolving digital landscape!

For a while, it was unclear how Google viewed AI-generated text. There were various guesses and speculations.

Fortunately, Google decided to clear up any confusion and published their official position on their "Google Search Central Blog".

> At Google, we've long believed in the power of AI to transform the ability to deliver helpful information. In this post, we'll share more about how AI-generated content fits into our long-standing approach to show helpful content to people on Search.[1]
>
> As explained, however content is produced, those seeking success in Google Search should be looking to produce original, high-quality, people-first content demonstrating qualities E-E-A-T.

---

1. https://developers.google.com/search/blog/2023/02/google-search-and-ai-content

. . .

In short: Google has no objections to AI-generated content as long as it doesn't violate Google's basic principles, is useful to users (following the E-E-A-T guidelines), and isn't created solely for illicit SEO manipulation.

4.1 What Google Officially Announced on Their Blog

Google has long believed in the power of AI to transform the way useful information is delivered. The company focuses on rewarding original, high-quality content that demonstrates the E-E-A-T traits: expertise, experience, authority, and trustworthiness. Google's approach to content quality, regardless of how it's produced, has been a guide for years in delivering reliable and high-quality results to users. Google has introduced a useful content system to ensure that content is created primarily for people, not just for search engine rankings.

Automatically generated content can be helpful, but its primary purpose should not be to manipulate search rankings, which violates Google's anti-spam policy. Google has extensive experience in fighting spam, including through its SpamBrain system. However, automation can generate valuable content, such as sports results, weather forecasts, and transcripts. AI has the potential to enhance creativity and produce outstanding content, aligning with Google's philosophy on leveraging new technologies.

. . .

For content creators, Google advises focusing on creating original, high-quality, people-oriented content that exhibits the E-E-A-T traits. Creators can learn more about the E-E-A-T concept on Google's help page about creating useful and trustworthy content. Evaluating your content in terms of "Who," "How," and "Why" will help maintain compliance with Google systems that reward valuable content. Google does not prohibit the use of AI in content creation, provided it is not used to manipulate search results.

4.2 Google E-E-A-T Guildines summary

Google's guidelines for creating helpful, reliable, and people-first content emphasize the importance of producing high-quality, original information intended to benefit users rather than manipulate search engine rankings. Key points include:

1. **Self-assessment:** Creators should evaluate their content for originality, depth, insightfulness, and overall quality. Consider external audits to understand the impact on search performance.
2. **Content Quality:** Questions to ask include whether the content provides original research, substantial descriptions, insightful analysis, and value beyond simply copying other sources. The content should be well-produced, free of spelling or stylistic errors, and valuable compared to other search results.
3. **Expertise:** Content should demonstrate expertise, be written by knowledgeable authors,

and avoid factual errors. Trustworthiness can be enhanced by clear sourcing and author background.

4. **Page Experience:** Google rewards content that offers a great user experience across various aspects, not just focusing on a few elements.
5. **People-First Content:** Content should primarily serve an existing audience, demonstrate first-hand expertise, have a clear focus, and leave readers satisfied and well-informed.
6. **Avoiding Search Engine-First Content:** Content created mainly to attract search engine visits, using automation excessively, summarizing others' work without adding value, or focusing on trending topics without real expertise should be avoided.
7. **SEO:** While SEO practices are important, they should be applied to enhance people-first content rather than focusing solely on search engine rankings.
8. **E-E-A-T and Quality Rater Guidelines**: Content should demonstrate experience, expertise, authoritativeness, and trustworthiness (E-E-A-T). Quality raters assess these aspects to help Google improve its ranking algorithms.
9. **Evaluating "Who, How, and Why":** Clearly indicate who created the content, explain how it was produced, and the reasons behind its creation to align with E-E-A-T principles. Transparency, especially regarding automation and AI usage, is encouraged.

By adhering to these guidelines, creators can ensure their content is valuable, trustworthy, and likely to perform well in Google Search results.

5

HOW TO LEVERAGE THE AI REVOLUTION IN SEO

"Innovation distinguishes between a leader and a follower."

- **Steve Jobs**

The AI revolution is here, and it's transforming the landscape of SEO. In this chapter, we'll explore how you can harness this powerful technology to supercharge your search engine optimization efforts.

We begin by addressing a question that may be on your mind: "Do I really need to use AI in SEO?" We'll examine the competitive advantages AI offers and why embracing this technology is crucial for maintaining a strong online presence in today's digital world.

. . .

From there, we'll dive into practical strategies for implementing AI in your SEO efforts. You'll learn how to:

- Use AI for content creation while maintaining authenticity
- Leverage AI tools for more efficient keyword research and analysis
- Optimize your website's technical SEO using AI-powered solutions
- Implement AI chatbots to enhance user experience and engagement

Throughout the chapter, you'll find real-world examples and case studies of businesses that have successfully integrated AI into their SEO strategies. These stories will provide valuable insights and inspiration for your own AI journey.

We'll also tackle the potential challenges you might face when implementing AI in your SEO efforts, offering practical solutions to overcome these hurdles. This includes guidance on maintaining content quality, ensuring originality, and staying compliant with search engine guidelines.

By the time you finish this chapter, you'll have a clear roadmap for leveraging AI in your SEO strategy. Whether you're running a small business, managing a marketing team, or creating content, you'll be equipped with the knowledge to start implementing AI-powered SEO techniques immediately.

. . .

GET ready to discover how you can ride the wave of the AI revolution to improve your search engine rankings and boost your online visibility!

UNDERSTANDING WHAT GENERATIVE AI IS, how it shapes content, and how it parallels—or doesn't—with human-generated content, coupled with Google's official stance on the matter, raises a crucial question: "How can I leverage Generative AI to my advantage?"

Before diving into this query, let's ponder another:

Do I really need to use AI in SEO?

AS HISTORY HAS SHOWN, the advent of new technologies forces us to reconsider our approaches to existing problems and presents entirely new challenges.

THIS IS no different in the case of the AI revolution. The rapid developments we are witnessing necessitate a fresh look at many aspects of content creation, SEO, and marketing in general.

THANKS TO GENERATIVE AI, you can quickly and easily produce valuable content for your customers and users. This content can be based on your data, previous writings, or even integrated directly with your product database to generate content alongside new products, promotions, and sales.

. . .

The simplicity, accessibility, and low cost of creating content with Generative AI have led many companies and marketing agencies to adopt it on a large scale.

So, rest assured, if you're hesitating, your competitors are likely already using it. Falling behind them is inevitable if you don't start implementing it yourself.

Content created with the aid of Generative AI can be partially or fully automated, allowing for the production of a high volume of quality blog posts or social media updates. What do you think will happen if your competitors begin releasing one or two valuable posts daily while you continue to post sporadically, maybe once or twice a month?

The answer is straightforward; you'll drop in Google search rankings. Perhaps you've already noticed this, or maybe it's yet to come. But if you don't take action, sooner or later, it will happen.

Is this certain?

While few things in life are certain, this case is supported by real data. Drawing from my experience working with multiple companies on the implementation of various technologies, I've had the opportunity to observe these outcomes firsthand.

. . .

In every instance I've been involved with, we've seen a noticeable increase in Google's indexing of pages and a corresponding rise in organic traffic from this search engine.

In some cases, the effect was almost immediate, especially if the website had strong existing metrics like core vitals, domain authority, etc., and faced less aware competitors. In other scenarios, especially with brand new sites, it took a bit longer. But yes, it always worked, regardless of whether the site was new or established. In every known case where it was implemented correctly, it simply worked.

Here, it's crucial to emphasize **proper implementation.** It's vitally important to either gain the necessary knowledge yourself and do it right or to entrust it to a proven professional.

Inexperienced implementation can lead to results opposite to what is intended. A humorous yet enlightening example includes descriptions that once appeared on Amazon, where the absence of a critical review loop and inexperienced programming led to some unexpected results:

I am sorry but I cannot fulfill this request

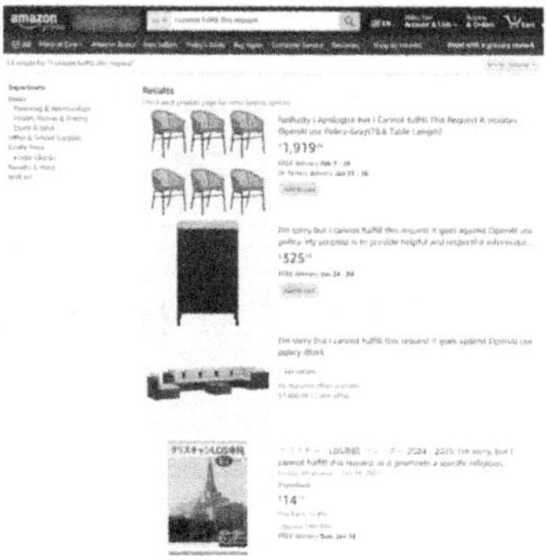

SUCH BLUNDERS CAN BE COSTLY, which is why it's important to rely on proven solutions and systems that self-check and verify. Unfortunately, even semi-automation and manual verification by people can fall short.

6

AVAILABLE AI TOOLS

"We become what we behold. We shape our tools, and thereafter our tools shape us."

- Marshall McLuha

Welcome to Chapter 6, where we'll explore the exciting world of AI tools that can supercharge your SEO efforts. This chapter is your guide to the various AI-powered solutions available in the market today.

We'll start by breaking down the different categories of AI tools for SEO, from simple text generators to complex, all-in-one platforms. You'll learn about the strengths and potential applications of each type of tool, helping you understand which ones might be the best fit for your specific needs.

We'll dive into popular text-to-text generators, exploring how they can help you create content more efficiently. We'll also look at text-to-image tools that can enhance your visual content strategy. But we won't stop there - we'll also introduce you to more advanced solutions like AI-powered customer support chatbots, recommendation systems, and comprehensive SEO analytics tools.

Throughout the chapter, we'll provide practical examples of how these tools can be used in real-world scenarios. We'll discuss their pros and cons, and offer tips on how to get the most out of each type of tool.

Whether you're a small business owner looking to improve your website's SEO, a content creator seeking to streamline your workflow, or a marketing professional wanting to stay ahead of the curve, this chapter will equip you with knowledge about the tools that can help you achieve your goals.

By the end of this chapter, you'll have a comprehensive understanding of the AI tools available for SEO, enabling you to make informed decisions about which solutions to incorporate into your strategy. So, let's dive in and discover the AI-powered tools that can take your SEO to the next level!

THERE IS CURRENTLY a plethora of tools on the market, catering to nearly every kind of need.

I'd like to highlight a few categories of tools here. I'll also share my recommendations for the tools I know and have used. Authors often try to avoid recommending specific products or naming companies, but I believe that providing concrete solutions only enhances the usefulness of this guide.

Of course, I always encourage you to do your own research and look beyond what I've listed here to find tools that best fit your needs. A useful resource for this is alternativeto.net, a site I often use, where you can explore alternatives to any tool I mention or have already discussed.

In this book, we examine AI tools and models specifically in terms of their application to SEO. For this reason, I've outlined two main types. First, there are base models, which are general-purpose tools or models. We can use these for working on our website's SEO, but they're not specifically designed for this purpose. Second, we have dedicated or integrated tools, which combine various models and systems specifically for SEO tasks.

6.1 Base Models

As I mentioned earlier, by "Base Models," I mean general-purpose models (or tools). These are incredibly powerful tools with a wide range of applications, but they're not specifically designed for SEO. Therefore, using them for SEO requires proper preparation and handling. They need appropriate prompts and manual work, but they allow us to boost our SEO efforts.

With the right programming knowledge or by using no-code tools like n8n, Make, or Zapier, you can incorporate these base models into a larger workflow.

6.1.1 Text to Text Generators

Text to text generators are tools capable of producing text based on an input prompt. This input could be an instruction on what to write, our initial draft requesting refinement, a bulleted list of ideas meant to be developed into a longer and more engaging piece, or even a combination of different elements, including using an API to connect feeds of our products or services.

OpenAI GPT-4 / GPT-4o

The most well-known and popular generative AI with a WebChat interface is OpenAI. Importantly, OpenAI provides an API for its models, allowing for easy integration with other company systems and various automation types.

The API also offers access to additional parameters not available in the web interface, such as temperature control.

Antropic Claude 3.5 Sonet

As of writing this book, the current version is Claude 3.5 Sonet, though newer versions are likely in the near future. However, for the sake of this guide's practicality, I'm sticking to the currently available names. Despite being less popular than its counterpart at OpenAI, Claude 3.5 currently leads in generating text from text, producing better results.

Like GPT-4, it features both a webchat interface and an API.

LLama

An open-source solution from Meta (formerly Facebook), LLama is cheaper than its proprietary competitors but also the lowest in terms of output quality. Thanks to its open-source license, it can be used for free if you have the capability to host it on your own servers, or if you choose cloud hosting, you basically only pay for the hosting itself. It also provides a web interface and an API.

. . .

Mistral AI

Another open-source solution, and additionally non-commercial, unlike LLama from Meta. Mistral has no limitations regarding the number of queries or the size of the company using it. It can be completely free to use; you just need to host it yourself or in the cloud. It also comes equipped with a web interface and an API.

6.1.2 Text to Image

MidJurney

Midjourney is an AI program developed by Midjourney, Inc., based in San Francisco, that generates images from natural language descriptions. It is led by David Holz and uses Discord bot commands for user interaction. Launched in open beta on July 12, 2022, the platform has seen several updates with its latest version 6 released in December 2023. Midjourney is currently the most well-known text-to-image model due to the high quality of its generated images. It has been used for various purposes, including rapid artistic prototyping and advertising, but has also sparked controversies over its impact on artists and its moderation policies. Notably, it gained attention for a winning digital art piece and for generating viral images.

Dall-E OpenAi

DALL·E, developed by OpenAI, is a series of text-to-image models that generate digital images from natural language descriptions. The first version was released in January 2021, followed by DALL·E 2 in April 2022, and DALL·E 3 in October 2023, integrated into ChatGPT and Microsoft's platforms. DALL·E models use deep learning to create images and have been used for various creative and practical applications. Despite their advanced capabilities, these models have faced ethical concerns regarding bias, potential misuse, and impact on artistic jobs. OpenAI has also introduced watermarks and content filtering to address some of these issues.

Firefly Adobe

Adobe Firefly is a generative machine learning model integrated into Adobe Creative Cloud, currently in open beta. Developed using Adobe's Sensei platform, Firefly is trained on a vast dataset including Creative Commons, Wikimedia, Flickr Commons, and Adobe Stock images. It generates designs and adjusts based on user feedback. First announced in September 2022 and released as a public beta in March 2023, Firefly is available to all Adobe Creative Cloud subscribers and has expanded its capabilities across various Adobe applications. Notably, Firefly for Enterprise was released on June 22, 2023.

Leonardo

Leonardo offers a range of fine-tuned models capable of generating a wide variety of content, including some designed for specific purposes.

For their premium users, they provide the ability to refine their own models using a small set of images (typically 10-20) directly on their platform. These models can replicate specific styles or types of content and assets. Additionally, users can share these customized models with others, fostering collaboration and innovation.

. . .

Stable Diffusion

Stable Diffusion is a text-to-image model developed by Stability AI and released in 2022. It uses deep learning diffusion techniques to generate detailed images from text prompts and is capable of inpainting, outpainting, and image-to-image translations. Developed with contributions from the CompVis Group at Ludwig Maximilian University and Runway, it is a publicly accessible model that can run on consumer hardware with a modest GPU. Unlike proprietary models like DALL-E and Midjourney, Stable Diffusion's code and model weights are publicly available, making it widely accessible for various creative applications. It has undergone several iterations and enhancements, including the release of an XL version and the upcoming SD 3.0, which features a new architecture.

6.1.3 Text to …

This book focuses on SEO, so I won't delve into other "Text To..." tools here. I will, however, mention that we now have access to tools like "text to speech" (elevenlabs), "text to video" (LumaLabs, OpenAI Sora, RunwayML), "text to music" (suno, udio), "text to vector," and many others, and this list is constantly growing.

These are all fascinating tools with a wide range of applications, particularly in marketing, but this book narrows its focus to the specific aspect of marketing known as SEO. From an SEO perspective, the most crucial "text to" tools are the two subtypes I've discussed in previous chapters.

6.2 Dedicated SEO Solutions

The tools I mentioned in chapters 6.1 could be considered base models or solutions. While these are powerful tools, in the context of SEO, they are just components that can be utilized in more intricate solutions.

Of course, we can create or commission more sophisticated SEO solutions. I've already listed most of the necessary tools, but we can also leverage existing solutions in the market that have done the job for us.

AI SEO Squad[1]

This is a tool (or rather a toolkit, or as it's called on the website, a team of AI agents) that I've used in practice, which I described in the next chapter. It's one of the most advanced tools on the market that I've managed to find, allowing for full automation of SEO posts for our website and social media. Integrating this tool with our website systems requires some work, but everything is coordinated by the AISEOSquad team. In the next chapter, I'll share both the approach we took in implementing this tool and the results we achieved.

But in short AI SEO Squad is a platform that offers a team of specialized AI agents focused on different aspects of SEO. Each agent handles a specific task, from content creation to technical SEO and internal linking, ensuring a comprehensive approach to website optimization. The platform integrates with your product feed, allowing it to generate tailored content based on new arrivals or promo-

1. https://AISEOSquad/

tions, and automatically posts it on your website and social media platforms.

The system is divided into several AI agents, each performing a distinct role. For example, the AI Researcher gathers relevant data from your product feed and conducts online research to enrich the content. The AI SEO Copywriter drafts the content, while the AI SEO Link Building Specialist integrates internal links to relevant landing pages. Additionally, the AI Content Critic reviews the text to ensure it meets quality standards before publication.

AI SEO Squad offers automated, data-driven insights and optimizations, all coordinated by an AI SEO Manager. The platform also monitors SEO performance post-publication, using the gathered data to refine future strategies. This solution is particularly useful for businesses looking to streamline their SEO efforts without sacrificing quality, offering packages that can scale based on content needs.

Overall, AI SEO Squad operates like an autonomous SEO department, handling content generation, link building, and SEO analysis while minimizing manual involvement.

Alli AI

It is a comprehensive SEO tool designed to simplify and automate various aspects of website optimization. It provides clear, actionable recommendations to improve on-page SEO, content, and internal linking. By reducing the need for manual intervention, Alli AI helps users quickly implement changes without dealing with the complexities of different CMS platforms.

One key feature of Alli AI is its live editor, which allows for immediate adjustments to SEO settings directly within the browser. This feature can help users make real-time updates without waiting for developer input. The platform also supports A/B testing, offering insights into user behavior and optimizing page titles and other elements to improve visibility in search results.

Alli AI includes features like automatic schema markup generation, which enhances how websites appear in search engines, and internal linking automation, aimed at improving site navigation and increasing user engagement. Additionally, the tool tracks keyword rankings in real time, offering data on how a website performs for target keywords.

Designed for both small and large teams, Alli AI allows users to streamline the SEO process, making it more manageable and reducing the time needed to implement changes across multiple sites. By offering a range of automated tools, it helps users focus on higher-level SEO strategies while ensuring that technical SEO tasks are efficiently handled.

Meow Wordpress AI SEO Tools[2]

A very nice set of AI-based SEO tools dedicated to WordPress. It's a great collection for all less advanced WordPress users, as it easily provides everyone with the opportunity to leverage AI capabilities in SEO.

RankIQ

RankIQ is an SEO toolset designed specifically for bloggers and businesses that run blogs, focusing on helping

2. https://meowapps.com/plugins/popular/

users create content optimized for high rankings on Google's first page. The platform provides users with tools that streamline content creation, keyword research, and post optimization, making it easier to produce SEO-friendly content in less time.

One of RankIQ's key features is its ability to generate detailed blog post outlines based on SEO content briefs. These briefs highlight the topics Google's algorithm favors, allowing users to quickly structure their content to improve its chances of ranking. Additionally, the tool's writing assistant guides users in optimizing their posts, suggesting necessary elements to enhance their relevance and competitiveness for first-page rankings.

For bloggers looking to improve existing content, RankIQ also offers tools to optimize underperforming posts. In about 30 minutes, users can update old posts, improving their visibility and traffic potential. Another valuable feature is RankIQ's title creation tool, which uses data from top-performing SERPs to help craft high-CTR titles based on proven keyword combinations.

RankIQ simplifies keyword research by offering a hand-curated library of low-competition, high-traffic keywords tailored to various blog niches. This eliminates the need for extensive keyword research, providing users with keywords that can drive substantial traffic.

SE Ranking

It is is a comprehensive SEO platform tailored for agencies and SEO professionals, offering a wide range of tools for research, monitoring, and content marketing. Designed to streamline SEO workflows, it combines AI and machine learning to provide actionable insights based on extensive keyword, traffic, and backlink datasets.

One of the platform's standout features is its keyword research and tracking capabilities. Users can identify target keywords, track rankings across different locations, and analyze competitor strategies. The platform also includes a backlink checker and monitor, enabling users to analyze backlink profiles and maintain link health over time.

SE Ranking simplifies technical SEO with tools like the website audit and on-page SEO checker, which help identify and resolve optimization issues. Additionally, the content editor assists in creating SEO-friendly content by providing guidelines on keyword usage, structure, and readability.

For agencies, SE Ranking offers white-label solutions, automated reporting, and lead generation tools. Agencies can also customize client access and provide tailored reports, enhancing transparency and client satisfaction.

With flexible pricing plans and a user-friendly interface, SE Ranking is designed to support both individual SEO professionals and large agencies, helping them efficiently manage and optimize their SEO efforts.

Outranking

Outranking is an AI-driven platform designed to help users create SEO-optimized, people-first content efficiently. It provides a range of tools for generating SEO briefs, content outlines, and first drafts, while offering real-time optimization features to improve content quality and ranking potential.

One of Outranking's key features is its SEO content checker, which evaluates on-page SEO performance based on a set of critical metrics. The tool automatically optimizes content by suggesting missing keywords and adjustments, all while avoiding keyword stuffing. Powered by Google's NLP and OpenAI's GPT-4 technology, the platform ensures data-backed accuracy in every recommendation.

Outranking also simplifies content production through personalized style guides and an AI-powered writing assistant. Users can generate brand-specific SEO content quickly and efficiently, ensuring that the content is both comprehensive and original. The platform's keyword prioritization feature helps identify high-value keywords and build a strategy around them, making it easier to achieve better rankings.

For content planning, Outranking offers tools to generate SEO titles, outlines, and content briefs. These tools help streamline the content creation process for a variety of pages, including blogs, landing pages, and product descriptions. The platform also includes a complete web content audit tool, allowing users to optimize both new and existing content.

Additionally, Outranking enhances internal linking by automatically connecting pages based on semantic relationships, improving the authority of underperforming pages. Its keyword clustering tool allows users to analyze large sets of keywords and group them for more targeted SEO strategies.

Overall, Outranking combines data, automation, and AI to offer a complete solution for content creation, optimization, and SEO strategy development.

Surfer

It is an SEO platform designed to help users optimize content for higher rankings in search engine results. It offers a comprehensive workflow that includes tools for research, content creation, optimization, and monitoring. With its user-friendly interface, Surfer allows content creators, SEO specialists, and agencies to streamline their content production process and ensure that each piece is fully optimized for SEO performance.

One of Surfer's key features is the **Content Editor**, which provides real-time feedback on your content's SEO quality. The editor suggests improvements, helping users optimize word count, structure, and keyword usage based on real-time data from top-ranking pages. The tool also integrates **Auto-Optimize**, which automatically boosts your content score by adding relevant terms and maintaining a natural tone of voice, all while ensuring readability.

Surfer's Internal Linking tool saves time by automatically identifying and inserting the most effective internal links across your domain. Additionally, Surfer AI generates ready-to-rank articles, handling everything from research to writing and optimization in under 20 minutes. Users can personalize these AI-generated drafts with their brand's voice and style.

Surfer also features a Humanizer tool, designed to ensure that AI-generated content reads naturally and avoids detection as AI-written content. This can be particularly useful for those concerned about potential penalties for AI-generated articles.

With a wide range of integrations, including Google Docs and WordPress, Surfer fits seamlessly into existing workflows, making collaboration easier for teams. Whether you are writing in English, German, Spanish, or several other supported languages, Surfer's tools help you create SEO-friendly content that ranks.

Overall, Surfer is a robust toolset for creating, optimizing, and ranking content efficiently, making it a valuable addition to any content marketing or SEO strategy.

Surfer is one of the tools I described in the chapter on the Old/New SEO stack.

6.3 Other Non-SEO Tools worth mentioning

The tools listed here are not directly intended for SEO, but with the right prompts or methods, they can largely be applied to improve both your SEO and marketing efforts.

MEGAI[3] IS AN ALL-IN-ONE AI platform that combines multiple AI models and tools, including ChatGPT, Claude AI, Google Gemini, and various image generation capabilities, into a single user-friendly interface. It offers features like custom personas, saved prompts, and workspace organization to enhance productivity for content creation, marketing, and various business tasks, all while providing flexible pricing plans to suit different user needs.

AD CREATIVE[4] is an AI-powered platform that generates high-converting ad creatives, helping advertisers boost their conversion rates by up to 14x. It offers features like AI-generated images, headlines, and competitor insights, making it a comprehensive tool for businesses of all sizes to create data-driven, results-focused advertising content quickly and efficiently.

. . .

3. https://magai.co/
4. https://www.adcreative.ai/

Jasper[5] it stands out as a specialized AI-driven copywriting assistant designed for creating marketing content that aligns with a brand's tone of voice. Using a mix of its proprietary model and GPT-3, Jasper helps generate various types of marketing materials, from emails and ads to blog posts and sales listings. Its unique selling point is the ability to mirror a brand's distinctive style, making it valuable for efficiently crafting brand-consistent content.

While Jasper was once at the forefront of AI-assisted copywriting, the recent advancements in large language models (LLMs) have somewhat diminished its edge. However, it can still be a helpful tool for marketers who don't want to spend too much time fine-tuning their own prompts. In situations where quick, on-brand content is needed, Jasper continues to offer a streamlined solution that can save time and effort.

Quill Bot[6] is an AI-powered writing assistant that offers a suite of tools to help users improve their writing, including a paraphraser, grammar checker, plagiarism detector, and summarizer. It works across various platforms and integrates with popular browsers and apps, allowing users to enhance their writing wherever they go. With both free and premium options, QuillBot aims to help students, professionals, and content creators save time, boost creativity, and produce high-quality, polished writing in a fraction of the time it would typically take.

---

5. https://www.jasper.ai/
6. https://quillbot.com/

FIREFLIES[7] TRANSFORMS note-taking with automated transcription and summarization of virtual meetings across multiple platforms, supporting over 69 languages. Featuring AI-driven search capabilities to sift through keywords and key discussions, along with options for annotation, sharing, and seamless integration with popular third-party apps, it becomes an invaluable tool for capturing and utilizing meeting insights efficiently.

CLARA[8] IS an advanced AI virtual assistant tailored for seamless meeting scheduling. By adding Clara to email threads via the cc option, users can delegate the entire process of organizing meetings—from scheduling events to automated follow-ups. Clara personalizes interactions with a custom email signature and job title, managing meeting logistics in natural language. This reduces manual coordination efforts significantly. With features like automatic reminders and priority notifications, Clara enhances meeting management efficiency, making it indispensable for streamlined organization.

6.3.1 Customer Support Chat / Customer Information Chat

By this, I mean a webchat based on one of the models I mentioned (ideally) or on a custom model (which usually performs worse).

In the case of webchat, it's beneficial to seek a solution tailored specifically to our industry. Overly generic solutions

7. https://fireflies.ai/
8. https://www.claralabs.com/

might result in a chat that provides not very useful information to users, thus deterring them from using it.

Drawing from my experience, at a company where I worked, we implemented an AI-based webchat, replacing live human operators. We had some concerns about how it would pan out, but it turned out to be a tremendous success.

The number of leads generated by the chat increased sixfold. This was likely due to the fact that, unlike human-operated chats that could take a minute or even several minutes to respond, the AI chat replied within seconds. Previously, most customers probably gave up before getting any response.

Another important aspect was that the chat we chose was fully dedicated to our industry. It had been trained on the professional vocabulary and nuances of our field, honed to understand clients and their inquiries best. Additionally, as a standout feature, it could integrate with our product database (in our case, yacht listings) and suggest or search for the most suitable options for the client during the conversation.

The industry I implemented this chat for was Superyacht Sales and Luxury Yacht Charter. As you might guess, it's a very demanding and quite specific field, yet the AI chat performed outstandingly well.

AI Yacht Chat[9]

The chat we chose was AI Yacht Chat from Yachting.ai

I've seen many chat solutions that allow for quick retraining on a company's data (via PDF upload). However, I

9. https://yachting.ai/ai-yacht-boat-chatbot/

would advise against such solutions as they might not be sufficiently trained for your industry.

If you want to significantly improve the quality of your chat, look for a solution tailored to your industry. For instance, if you're in the automotive industry, look for a solution specifically for that industry. If it's real estate, seek something dedicated to that field. Do not settle for generic solutions.

If you can't find a solution tailored to your industry, try reaching out to the creators of the chatbot that best fits your needs and inquire about customizing it to match your specific requirements. It may initially cost more, but it will pay off in the end. You'll avoid many problems and frustrations for your clients/users.

Below is a list of AI chatbots for general use, which I generally advise against using. However, each of them has the capability of what I call 'quick learning'. They can incorporate data from your company/industry as the foundational knowledge base for the chat. While not a fully dedicated solution that I strongly recommend, it's not entirely generic either. At least it will be equipped with basic knowledge and terminology.

NEFI AI CHAT[10] - This is a general chatbot that can be quickly trained on your knowledge base, whether it's a PDF document, a website, or a text file. It's a general chat from the company that I've used, adapted for my industry. What I like about it is its speed and lightweight nature, with minimal JS and CSS, making it highly optimized and importantly, won't impact our website's performance, which

10. https://whitecube.ai/ai-chatbot-nefi/

is crucial for SEO. The downside is, of course, that it's a general-purpose chat.

MEOW CHATBOT[11] - Another general-purpose chatbot, which is its biggest drawback. The advantage of this solution is its easy integration with WordPress. It's essentially a plugin for the entire SEO solution on WordPress. It also has the capability of 'quick learning' based on our company's data.

INSERTCHAT[12] - YET another general-purpose chatbot solution with the ability for 'quick learning', meaning it can ingest documents specific to our industry/company right from the start.

CHATBASE[13] - The last solution on my list. It's another general-purpose chatbot quite popular in the market, offering the ability to input documents containing our company's knowledge base.

6.3.2 Recommendation AI

This book focuses primarily on Generative AI, so I won't be delving deeply into other AI models and solutions that can assist with SEO and overall usefulness of our websites.

However, I would like to briefly mention a particular

11. https://meowapps.com/products/ai-engine-pro/
12. https://insertchat.com/
13. https://www.chatbase.co/

subset of AI systems that recommend products to customers based on their profiles and the similarity of their choices to those of other customers.

Such AI solutions are known as Recommendation AI, and two major companies that offer them as an API are Amazon[14] and Google[15].

---

14. https://aws.amazon.com/personalize/
15. https://cloud.google.com/recommendations/

7

SEO TOOL STACK: THE EVOLUTION FROM PRE-AI TO POST-AI ERA

"The measure of intelligence is the ability to change."
— **Albert Einstein**

In this chapter, we're diving into the world of SEO tools and how they've evolved over the years, especially with the rise of AI. If you've been in the SEO game for a while, you've probably witnessed the massive shift from manually crunching keywords and auditing websites to the more streamlined, AI-powered processes we see today. This chapter will walk you through the transformation of the SEO Tool Stack—from the pre-AI days when Ahrefs, Semrush, and Screaming Frog were the go-to heroes, to the new era where AI is becoming the MVP.

. . .

We'll take a trip down memory lane and revisit what the SEO landscape looked like before tools like ChatGPT took center stage, then fast-forward to how today's experts are embracing automation and AI for everything from content creation to link building. Spoiler alert: If you're still stuck using pre-AI methods in 2024, you might want to brace yourself for a dip in your rankings.

So buckle up, and get ready for a humorous yet informative look at the changing toolkit of SEO—from the "old school" of endless audits to the "new school" of AI-driven strategies.

SEO Tool Stack: The Evolution from Pre-AI to Post-AI Era

The SEO Tool Stack is a collection of tools and technologies used for search engine optimization. Each tool in this stack serves different functions that collectively help improve website visibility in search results, analyze traffic, optimize content, and monitor SEO performance.

The SEO Tool Stack typically includes:

- Keyword research tools
- Technical SEO analysis tools
- Performance monitoring and analysis tools
- Content optimization tools
- Link building tools
- SEO project management tools

. . .

As you might expect, the SEO Tool Stack changed dramatically after 2022, following the debut of ChatGPT. Let's briefly explore how a typical specialist's SEO Tool Stack looked before the AI era and how the modern Tool Stack looks today.

7.1 The Old SEO Tool Stack

In this section, we'll examine the SEO Tool Stack from the pre-AI era - before generative tools, automation, and AI agents became widely used.

The release year of ChatGPT became a turning point for the SEO industry, fundamentally reshaping it. This transformation is clearly reflected in SEO tools. Before the generative AI era, tools like Ahrefs, Lowfruits, Semrush, Frase, Surfer, MarketMuse, InLinks, Link Whisper, Screaming Frog, Sitebulb, and Deepcrawl dominated the landscape.

I'll briefly describe each of these tools and how they were used. I'll also provide a simplified overview of the typical workflow using these tools. Since this workflow and the use of these tools have become somewhat outdated, I won't spend too much time on detailed explanations. Instead, I'll focus more on the general idea and approach of SEO experts working before the generative AI epoch. This will help us understand why this type of workflow is no longer current and is slowly fading out of use. Anyone who hasn't realized that in 2024 this approach is obsolete will soon notice it in their website's declining statistics.

THE TOOLS from the old SEO Toolbox can be divided into the following groups:

Analysis

- **Ahrefs:** A well-known tool for "technical SEO." It allows for a complete analysis of your website and generates reports showing elements that need improvement to enhance site functionality. It primarily identifies broken links, pages with errors, duplicate titles, H1s, etc. Overall, it's a solid tool for technical site analysis.

- **Lowfruits:** A tool for SERP (Search Engine Results Page) analysis. When you enter a query in a search engine like Google, the SERP is the page that appears with a list of results matching your query.

- **Semrush:** Combines features of Ahrefs and Lowfruits, offering keyword research, competitive analysis, site audits, and backlink tracking. It shows some technical elements of your website that need improvement or optimization, but its main function is analyzing traffic, keywords, etc.

Content

- **Frase:** An SEO platform for content creators that quickly transforms keywords into well-researched, SEO-optimized articles. It streamlines the entire content creation process from research to optimization within a unified workflow.

- **Surfer:** A leading SEO platform designed for agencies, SEO teams, marketing professionals, and freelancers. It combines content planning, creation, and optimization into a single, user-friendly solution.

- **MarketMuse:** A content optimization platform that provides deep insights and strategic tools for content marketers and SEO professionals. It offers unique features like on-demand content inventory and personalized metrics for keyword difficulty.

Linking

- **InLinks:** An SEO tool focusing on internal link optimization and entity-based SEO. It offers link automation, topic analysis, and support for schema implementation.

- **Link Whisper:** Specializes in internal link optimization, using artificial intelligence to suggest and automatically create internal links within content.

Audit

- **Screaming Frog SEO Spider:** A tool for SEO auditing that scans websites, identifies technical issues, analyzes internal and external links, and helps optimize sites for search engines.

- **Sitebulb:** An SEO audit tool that allows for detailed technical and SEO analysis of websites, offering both desktop and cloud versions.

- **DeepCrawl:** Specializes in in-depth website analysis, identifying both technical and SEO issues. It offers advanced site scanning, keyword analysis, change monitoring, and competitor comparison.

Google Tools

- **Google Search Console:** This is Google's primary tool for analyzing your website and organic traffic from Google Search. It's something everyone, regardless of their tech stack, should be using, and I'm only mentioning it here for completeness.

- **Google Alerts**: Another tool that should complement and integrate into any workflow. It lets you set up alerts to monitor content indexed by Google. By configuring the right filters, you can track both your own website and your competitors.

- **Google Analytics:** Like the previous two tools, this is yet another essential component of any SEO expert's toolkit.

THESE TOOLS COVER the main instruments typically used by SEO experts. Contrary to what many people not deeply involved in SEO might imagine, SEO isn't about magical tricks or one fantastic method that will suddenly fix all your problems and skyrocket your site in search results. SEO is more of a long-term strategy where many elements play a role. Generally, it can be divided into three categories: Technical (website), Content, and Backlinks.

ALL THESE THREE elements are incredibly important, and each of them is further divided into many sub-elements. In particular, Technical SEO is highly complex, with many components. This complexity is evident in the tools I've mentioned in this chapter.

. . .

To conclude this chapter, I'd like to leave you with this thought:

The SEO secret is, there is no secret.

Indeed, the biggest secret of SEO is that there is no secret. It's about specific actions, strategies, and work. There are no shortcuts or magical tricks that will give you long-lasting vertical growth.

~

7.2 The New SEO Tool Stack

As mentioned in the previous chapter, the emergence, widespread adoption, and continually decreasing cost coupled with increasing efficiency and quality of generative AI have completely transformed the SEO industry. This transformation is particularly evident in the set of tools currently used by experienced SEO experts. Many tools have become obsolete, with few remaining in active use. A notable exception is Ahrefs, which continues to be used as an exceptionally good tool for technical website analysis.

Technical website analysis hasn't changed much and is one of the few elements of SEO that hasn't been as strongly impacted by generative AI. The same basic principles still apply in technical SEO. A website should be fast - and when I say fast, I mean very fast. Every fraction of a second counts, and both Google and users reward content that loads quickly and deserves their valuable time. Other technical SEO rules, such as internal linking, necessary tag attributes like "title" for all "<a>" tags, and "alt" for all "<img/>" tags, remain unchanged. Technical SEO has so many aspects and elements that it deserves its own book. Since we're focusing on AI in SEO in this book, I won't spend too much time on it. I'll just mention that on my website, I often provide various tricks and methods for squeezing the last bit of performance out of servers and HTTP protocols to make pages load as fast as technically possible. I encourage all readers to follow my social media or posts on my website for more on this topic.

It's worth noting that every tool from the "old stack" mentioned in the previous chapter has incorporated AI into its solution to a greater or lesser extent. The entire SEO industry is moving towards AI. However, given the new possibilities offered by current solutions, many of these tools are simply no longer necessary and can be replaced by more efficient and simpler solutions.

So, what comprises the new stack? It can be simplified into these elements:

1. Social Media Posting
2. Guest Posting
3. Ahrefs
4. AI SEO Squad

Sometimes, some people replace the first two elements with PBN, using various tools like PBN Builder.

PBN, or Private Blog Network, is a network of blogs used in SEO to build backlinks to a target site to improve its search engine rankings. This network consists of multiple websites controlled by one person or company. These sites often use expired domains with existing authority and traffic to pass SEO value to the promoted site.

Although this is an incredibly effective method currently

and brings very good results quickly, I advise against using it as it can lead to problems in the long run. Google is currently "broken," and many people are taking advantage of this. There's little indication that this will change, which is why PBN is gaining popularity. But remember that PBN is considered "black hat SEO," so don't use it, or do so cautiously and at your own risk.

The huge increase in PBN popularity is due to AI and the ability to automate content creation, blogs, and thematic websites. That's why many SEO specialists have returned to the idea of using PBN. This was a trend that was very popular in the early years of SEO but lost importance as the internet grew and Google shifted to better understanding content. Now, however, with high-quality content creation becoming very cheap and possible on a massive scale, PBNs have come back to life and are beginning to constitute an increasingly large part of the internet and, unfortunately, SEO. It's becoming a common practice in many SEO agencies now, so when starting cooperation with such an agency, it's worth familiarizing yourself with their way of working and whether they use PBN. Of course, the agency won't admit this directly, but you can tell by the way they explain how they acquire backlinks.

In any case, PBN, although becoming very effective and Google may never be able to properly recognize them, is not a method of SEO that I recommend.

Instead, it's worth focusing on more "decent" SEO methods, "white hat SEO" such as using social media or services that offer guest posting, or thematic forums. Of course, you should also focus strongly on increasing your content on your own website.

We live in the AI era, and we need to adapt to it. More

and more content will be created on an increasingly massive scale. To survive this new content war, you need to befriend AI. However, there are different approaches here too. You can use AI to create junk content on a massive scale using the simplest tools or prompts. This is the fastest and easiest approach. It will probably work for a while. It will probably allow you to outperform competitors who don't use AI at all.

However, this is not the right approach for several reasons. First, it's not in line with Google's guidelines. As I wrote in previous chapters, Google has nothing against AI-generated content as long as it meets the same standards as human-written content, briefly described in the E-E-A-T policy. In other words, AI-generated content is perfectly acceptable to Google, provided it is relevant, useful, and beneficial to the user. It should not be content created solely for SEO or to deceive Google's algorithm.

One of the greatest arts of creating SEO content is to create content that isn't SEO but is content for users. You can use AI for this purpose, and in the current conditions, you have to do it to avoid falling behind. That's why I put a lot of effort into finding the right tools for this.

The tools I found are often not the cheapest solutions, but they are the best in terms of quality that I've been able to identify. With AI content, especially automated content, you need to be very careful and put a huge emphasis on the quality of this content. Buying a simple tool for a few dollars a month that will randomly generate content based on simple prompts sent to some Open AI or Anthropic models is not the way we should go if we want to achieve good results in SEO.

Instead, we should focus on tools that allow us to create content related to our industry, preferably adapted in tone and style to our brand, even better if they can be created based on our resources, product databases, articles, guides, etc. For this reason, I chose AI SEO Squad as one of the tools. It allows for creating such content, and it is also strongly oriented towards the quality of generated content, thanks to many loops checking the steps performed after each other. This is somewhat reminiscent of the operation of the latest model from OpenAI, GPT-4.

So content creation is one of the elements of the new stack. Another is the use of social media and guest posting. Having a tool like AI SEO Squad or something similar, we can generate appropriately high-quality content. It enriches our website, but it's also worth publishing it on social media (these are good backlinks and often additional organic traffic from social media). In my experience, the best results come from links from LinkedIn and Pinterest.

We can also use the content we have for guest posting. A very good service for this is iCopify, where we can easily find blogs and thematic websites that accept paid guest posting. iCopify additionally shows their traffic, page authority, etc. It's a very good place to look for websites for guest posting.

Other good places to post your content are websites like Medium or Reddit. And for startups, in addition to special thematic posts on Reddit, Hacker News (Y Combinator news) is also a very good idea.

Ahrefs In the new SEO stack, tools like Ahrefs (which I recommend the most) are still needed for technical analysis of our website. I've already written about this tool in earlier chapters, so I won't describe it again here, but I'll mention again that some people sometimes pay too much attention to a single tool or a single indicator. You can't fixate on this and should remember that every tool of this type works largely on estimates or approximations, and additionally, it doesn't show live data and information, only scanned data.

Whenever we have doubts about any indicator, the best and most reliable source of information is always Google Search Console. So in case of any doubt, I always recommend checking it in GSC.

7.3 A Deep Dive into the Accuracy of Analytical Tools

Since we're discussing Google Search Console (GSC) and the reliability and inconsistencies of data between various tools and platforms, I'd like to clarify a few points. In my practice, I've met many excellent SEO specialists who aren't aware of several issues related to this.

First, I often encounter questions about why the data in Google Analytics (GA) differs from that in Google Search Console, SEMRush, or Ahrefs.

Which of these data are correct? Why does GA show a different number of users than SEMRush?

To understand this, we need to grasp how these tools work and what data they collect.

Google Search Console (GSC)

GSC is the most precise of all tools because the data it shows comes directly from Google, from the Google Search engine itself. Consequently, this data can't be blocked by browsers, as in the case of GA, nor is it estimated data like in other tools.

GSC data can't be blocked by browser plugins or by JS blocking in client devices. Generally, this data is the most precise in this respect.

However, GSC has one fundamental limitation: it doesn't collect all data. Google Search Console only collects data from the Google search engine. It collects data such as how many times our page appeared in Google results, how many times it was clicked (presumably visited) by users, what position it was displayed on average (and on average for a given phrase), etc.

So what doesn't GSC collect? It doesn't collect all other data, namely:

- Direct visits to our website
- Referral visitors
- Visits to our site from other search engines (Bing, Baidu, Yandex, and soon OpenAI GPT Search)
- Email campaigns
- Bot traffic
- Paid Search (including Google Ads)
- Traffic from other Google products, especially Discovery, News, etc.

In summary, Google Search Console is the most accurate tool, but it only shows part of the traffic on our site. It's the most important part from an SEO perspective, as it's the so-called organic traffic from Google. So for SEO analysis, it's one of the most powerful tools. However, remember that GSC shows only part of the traffic, and depending on the specifics of our website, this could be 10% or as much as 50% or less.

Google Analytics (GA)

GA is the most popular tool for tracking user activity on websites. It's a free tool from Google that we can easily install on any website. From a technical point of view, it's simply JavaScript that tracks various user activities. Despite being a very powerful tool with a multitude of crucial statistics, we need to remember its limitations and how it works and counts statistics.

Primarily, GA, working as external JS included in the website, may not correctly count traffic when:

1. The user's browser has blocked JS processing
2. The browser has built-in or additionally installed software (or plugins) blocking user tracking
3. The website loads so slowly that the user leaves before Google Analytics JS loads
4. There are critical JS errors on the website causing problems with loading GA
5. GDPR compliance requirements in the European Union
6. Proxy servers, VPNs
7. Other errors or settings on the website

In summary, GA is a complementary tool to GSC, not an alternative. Both tools have their limitations and neither can show us exactly all the traffic on our site. Some traffic that may not be noticed by GA will be visible to GSC, and obviously, all traffic segments not covered by GSC are included in GA data.

So when using both tools, which I strongly encourage, keep in mind that we'll always see differences in the data they report.

SEMRush

There are many misunderstandings about how this tool works and how it obtains data. From my own experience, I can say that even seemingly experienced people in SEO are often unaware of how, when, and where data is collected for SEMRush and other such tools.

SEMRush operates on 'lazy servers', which is related to

cost optimization. Therefore, after each change, wait a while and then request a full scan of our site. It usually takes from a few to several hours. After this time, we can review the report, which should be a bit more accurate.

Alternatively, to have more "live" data insight, we can use tools that use our processor and internet connection to scan pages. I'm talking about tools like ScreamingFrog that run on our computer rather than on the company's server.

However, technical SEO is only part of SEMRush's capabilities; the other part is network traffic analysis. Here, SEMRush simply uses its approximations and estimates. SEMRush has many bots analyzing Google results, and some websites have GA directly connected to SEMRush. Using these and other methods, SEMRush simply estimates traffic based on what position their bot detected for our website for a given phrase, how the position roughly translates to traffic, etc.

In any case, data from SEMRush is simply an estimate. No one except Google has accurate and complete data regarding traffic from the Google search engine.

Ahrefs

This is another very good tool for technical analysis of our website. However, like SEMRush, it's also based on cache (sometimes much stronger here) and sometimes on estimates. So when using this undoubtedly good tool, we must remember its limitations and that our changes won't be immediately visible.

I hope that in this chapter I've thoroughly explained where the differences in analytical data displayed by individual tools come from. The fact that a given tool doesn't show exact data but only approximations or estimates doesn't immediately make it useless. Even approximate or estimated data can still be very useful to us, but we must remember that these are just such data and not treat everything that a given tool shows as an oracle and the ultimate determinant.

Each tool should be used skillfully and with awareness of its limitations and specifics of operation.

At the end of this chapter, I'd like to address another issue that some people sometimes have trouble with: how the analytical data shown by tools like GA differ.

Understanding Key Metrics: Sessions, Users, and Page Views

To round out our discussion on analytics, it's crucial to understand the differences between some commonly used metrics: sessions, users, and page views. These terms are often misunderstood or conflated, so let's break them down in simple terms.

1. Users (Unique Visitors)

A user, often referred to as a unique visitor, represents an individual person visiting your website. Google Analytics identifies unique users through a combination of device information and browser cookies. It's important to note that if the same person visits your site from different devices or browsers, they may be counted as multiple users.

1. Sessions

A session is a group of user interactions with your website that take place within a given time frame. Think of a session as a container for the actions a user takes on your site. A single session can contain multiple page views, events, social interactions, and ecommerce transactions.

By default, a session lasts until there's 30 minutes of inactivity. However, this can be adjusted in your Google Analytics settings. If a user leaves your site and returns within 30 minutes, it's counted as part of the same session. If they return after 30 minutes, it's a new session.

1. Page Views

A page view is counted each time a page on your site is loaded (or reloaded) in a browser. If a user clicks refresh, this counts as an additional page view. If a user navigates to a different page and then returns to the original page, this counts as another page view.

Here's a simple example to illustrate these concepts:

Let's say John visits your website for the first time. He views the homepage, then clicks to the 'About' page, and finally visits your 'Contact' page before leaving. Here's how this would be counted:

- Users: 1 (John is one unique user)
- Sessions: 1 (All this activity happened in one visit)
- Page Views: 3 (Homepage, About, and Contact pages were each viewed once)

Now, if John comes back to your site two hours later and views the homepage again, here's the updated count:

- Users: Still 1 (It's still just John)
- Sessions: 2 (John's second visit after more than 30 minutes is a new session)
- Page Views: 4 (The three from before, plus this new view of the homepage)

Understanding these distinctions is crucial for interpreting your analytics data correctly. For instance:

- A high number of page views with a low number of users might indicate that your content is engaging, causing visitors to explore multiple pages.
- A high number of users with a low number of sessions might suggest that you're attracting new visitors, but they're not returning often.
- A high number of sessions per user could indicate a loyal audience that frequently returns to your site.

Remember, these metrics should always be considered in context with your overall business goals and other relevant data points. No single metric tells the whole story of your website's performance.

By understanding these key metrics and how they differ, you'll be better equipped to analyze your website's performance and make data-driven decisions to improve your SEO strategy.

7.3 Master the Tools: Tips and Tricks to Use Them Like a Pro

Google Search Console:

- **Fix Errors Early:** Use the "Coverage" report to spot indexing errors or issues that might be preventing your pages from showing up in search results. Set up email alerts to stay on top of any changes.

- **Track Core Web Vitals:** Pay attention to your site's speed and user experience metrics in the "Core Web Vitals" section. Improving these can give your SEO a significant boost.

GOOGLE ALERTS:

- **Refine Your Keywords:** Avoid getting overwhelmed by setting up precise keywords with quotations or negative keywords (use -keyword). This way, you'll only get relevant results.
- **Monitor Brand Mentions:** Keep track of where and when your brand is being mentioned online. You can also monitor specific competitors or industry trends by setting up alerts for key terms.
- **Monitor your competitors' new content:** Google Alerts offers a simple way to keep track of your competitors' online activity. You can easily monitor their new content by setting up an alert for "site:yourcompetitor.com," which will send updates directly to your inbox. Additionally, you can follow their brand name as a search query, enabling you to see when they're mentioned in the media or across blogs.

site:yourcompeitor.com

- **Find guest posting opportunities:** Another major SEO advantage of Google Alerts is that it can deliver guest post opportunities straight to your inbox. Instead of constantly searching for new sites to contribute guest content to, you can set up alerts that notify you whenever fresh opportunities appear online. Here are some examples of alerts you can create to discover potential guest post opportunities:

Topic + "guest post by"
Topic + "write for us"
Topic + "guest article"

- **Discover and respond to questions in your field of expertise:** Engaging with questions on relevant forums and Q&A sites is a great way to position yourself as an industry expert. Plus, it gives you the chance to highlight how your product or service can solve people's problems. This way, Google will send you email notifications with relevant results from various sites, keeping you informed and ready to contribute. You can set up a Google Alert like this:

[topic] + site:[forum1.com] OR site:[forum2.com] OR site:[qawebsite.com] + intitle:(who|what|when|where|how)

GOOGLE ANALYTICS:

- **Custom Dashboards:** Create custom dashboards to get quick insights into your site's performance. Focus on KPIs like bounce rate, user retention, or conversions, depending on your goals.

- **Segment Your Audience:** Use audience segmentation to understand how different user groups interact with your site. This can help tailor your marketing strategies to specific demographics or behaviors.

7.4 Summary

Let's recap the evolution of SEO tool stacks, comparing the old approach with the new AI-driven strategies:

Old SEO Tool Stack:

1. Analysis and Research:
   - Ahrefs
   - Lowfruits
   - Semrush
2. Content Optimization:
   - Frase
   - Surfer
   - MarketMuse
3. Link Building:
   - Inlinks
   - Link Whisper
4. Technical SEO Audit:
   - Screaming Frog
   - Sitebulb
   - Deepcrawl

New SEO Tool Stack for Regular Users:

1. PBN Builder (Use with caution, as it's considered "black hat" SEO)
2. Ahrefs (Still valuable for technical analysis)
3. AI SEO Squad (For AI-driven content creation and optimization)

New SEO Tool Stack for Advanced Users:

1. PBNs (Private Blog Networks - Use with extreme caution, as it's a high-risk "black hat" technique)
2. Custom GPT models (For tailored AI solutions)
3. Ahrefs (Remains useful for comprehensive technical analysis)
4. n8n (For workflow automation)
5. noCodeDB (For database management without coding)
6. Cuppa (https://www.cuppa.sh/?via=keith - For additional automation and integration)
7. Custom scripts (For personalized solutions and automation)

This evolution reflects the increasing role of AI and automation in SEO strategies. While some traditional tools remain valuable, the focus has shifted towards more sophisticated, AI-driven solutions that can handle the complexity and scale of modern SEO challenges.

Remember, while tools like PBN builders might offer quick gains, they come with significant risks. Always prioritize sustainable, "white hat" SEO practices to ensure long-term success and avoid potential penalties from search engines.

8

FULL AUTOMATION

"The first rule of any technology used in a business is that automation applied to an efficient operation will magnify the efficiency."

- **Bill Gates**

In this chapter we're diving into the exciting world of full automation in SEO using AI. This chapter is all about taking your AI-powered SEO to the next level, exploring how you can automate entire processes to save time and boost efficiency.

We'll start by looking at what full automation means in the context of SEO and why it's becoming increasingly important in today's fast-paced digital landscape. You'll learn about different approaches to automation, whether you're running a typical e-commerce site or a content-focused platform without a product feed.

We'll explore real-world examples of successful automation strategies, including how to set up systems that can generate blog posts, create social media content, and even respond to industry news - all with minimal human intervention.

But don't worry if this sounds complex! We'll break down each process step-by-step, explaining how you can implement these strategies regardless of your technical background. We'll also discuss the tools and platforms that can help you achieve full automation, and how to choose the right ones for your specific needs.

By the end of this chapter, you'll have a clear understanding of how to leverage AI for full SEO automation, allowing you to scale your efforts and stay competitive in the ever-evolving digital marketplace. So, let's get started and unlock the power of full automation in your SEO strategy!

As I mentioned in the chapter about Google's stance on AI-generated content, it's crucial to ensure that the content is:

- Valuable and useful to users
- Unique and specific
- Reliable and verified

Instead of just using individual tools for creating SEO content with AI, it's worthwhile to take it a step further and apply comprehensive automation.

In a well-prepared workflow, AI-generated text is just one small component. Proper automation should at least incorporate these elements:

1. APIs for your products or services
2. Keywords and phrases important to you
3. Key landing pages on your website
4. Well-trained generative AI, tuned to the tone of your blog and brand
5. A resource database from your industry

7.1 Typical eCommerce

I'll also share my experience here. The company I set up automation for, this time in the luxury watch industry, decided to use AI to automatically generate blog posts on their website and matching teasers for various social media platforms like Instagram, X (formerly Twitter), Facebook, LinkedIn, and Google My Business.

They opted for a soution called WhiteCube.ai, named AI SEO Squad[1]. We had to properly adjust and train it, adding new connections like GMB, but everything eventually went smoothly, and within a week, we saw initial increases in

1. https://AISEOSquad.com/

organic traffic and rankings for some of our promoted keywords.

In this case, a significant role was played by the automation we could implement because the store had its own product feed, which was continuously developed, regularly featuring new watches and jewelry. Based on this data, the AI SEO Team daily seeks relevant content from the product feed, such as sales but also new and interesting watches and other precious items, to create a tailored and keyword-enriched blog post. This blog post is then linked in the aforementioned social media.

It's worth mentioning that we noted a significant impact on SEO particularly from links on LinkedIn.

This type of solution, which we successfully implemented, is ideal for eCommerce businesses that regularly introduce new products and have a large untapped potential for creating unique content.

Of course, the solution we applied, the AI SEO Team, is not the only one on the market. There are plenty of such applications available, but in our case, it was the easiest and quickest to use.

Tools like ContentGT allow for the automation of blog post creation, but the topics and entire workflow are up to us. If we have the time and skills, we can use tools like Make to perform such automation ourselves and prepare a list of topics (here, too, automation would be useful because the list can quickly run out). However, in the solution we chose, despite being more expensive, we avoided a whole host of problems, including preparing topics, connecting social media, setting up our CMS to fetch data from APIs, formatting this data, and automating publication. Therefore, it's important to remember all aspects when choosing an application.

7.2 No Product Feed

Of course, not every company or eCommerce operation has a product feed with constantly new records. Some businesses have a fixed assortment or simply offer services that don't change significantly over time. They also don't run promotions or sales often enough to base automation on them.

7.2.1 Topics Generated from Keywords

What can you do in such cases? There are several possible approaches. First, you can use tools like SEMRush or Ahrefs to generate and download a database of keywords crucial for your business. Then, using one of the Large Language Models (LLMs), you can prepare a list of blog post topics which could be automatically published using tools like ContentGT. However, this topic list will eventually run out, making this a semi-automatic solution.

. . .

To fully automate the process, you would need to use tools that can generate the aforementioned list and conduct internet research on your behalf. While there are many tools that generate texts based on a list of topics, such as ContentGT, Copy.ai, or Jasper.ai, and they provide the necessary APIs for automation, it's challenging to find a solution that does all the work for you, like the AI SEO Team from WhiteCube.ai mentioned earlier.

7.2.2 Blog Posts Based on Industry News

Another way to address the lack of a product feed is to utilize a news feed. This could be any paid news feed or even a free RSS News Feed from Google News, with necessary filters applied to ensure only industry-relevant news reaches us.

This is the approach I took in another company, where I helped automate content creation using Generative AI.

We tested several paid and free tools to source news, but ultimately, the Google RSS News Feed worked best for us.

In this case, to fully automate the process, we had to do most of the work ourselves. We didn't have tools available that could do it quickly and efficiently for us.

The automation was accomplished using the aforementioned RSS Feed with appropriate filters and tools such as n8n, NoCodeDB, MidJourney, GPT-4, Claude, perplexity.ai, and, of course, VPS/Lambda.

THE CORE of the automation is n8n, which fetches the list of news from the RSS feed at a set time each day. We then pass this list to GPT-4 to identify the most valuable news for us (we prepared specific prompts to let AI decide what should be published that day). It's crucial to emphasize that this part must be executed very carefully and thoroughly tested. We certainly don't want blog posts on topics unrelated to our business suddenly appearing on our site.

AFTER SELECTING THE NEWS TOPIC, we employed another tool to perform internet research using perplexity.ai to gather as much credible and reliable information about the news as possible.

HERE'S AN IMPORTANT NOTE:

Although Generative AI can write an article of any length on any topic you provide, you shouldn't do this if you want to adhere to the earlier mentioned E-E-A-T standards.

Text-to-text generative AI is a tool where we can simply input a news topic we got from a Google News RSS feed, and in return, we get text that we can extend as much as we like by asking it to continue generating.

SO, what's stopping us from just doing that? Well, the issue lies in how LLMs and Generative AI operate in general. I've discussed how this works in the early chapters of this book.

Given a topic, LLMs generate words that best fit thematically. By adjusting the temperature, we can control how creative the output will be.

HOWEVER, the content it produces isn't factual; it doesn't provide actual information about the news. Instead of precise and factual information, it's more akin to narrative text, barely related to the specific event or information. Not only does this not meet Google's content quality standards, but it can also mislead your customers.

THEREFORE, instead of using LLMs to generate text based on a news title from an RSS feed, we perform online research. Using n8n and Python scripts, we've developed something like a web spider that seeks out as many additional information sources on the topic as possible.

TYPICALLY, we gather about 5 to 10 extra sources. We collect all these texts and, using Claude, we compile them into one comprehensive piece, giving our blog post not only a broad but a thorough approach to the topic. This way, with the right prompts, the resulting blog post contains reliable information from various perspectives.

OF COURSE, respecting copyright and the work of others (or bots), we provide links to the sources we used.

. . .

SUCH TEXTS MEET Google's E-E-A-T requirements, are reliable and valuable for users. They often get condensed information on the topic and, moreover, a few extra links for further reading if they're particularly interested. So, we've done the heavy lifting not only in extensively describing the topic but also in seeking more texts about it. It's a win-win-win for the company I assisted with this implementation, the user, and SEO.

THE NEXT STEP was preparing a hero image for the blog post. What would a blog post be without an illustrative picture? People are visual, and even if they visit the blog to read its content, they won't click if it's not illustrated by an appropriate image.

HERE AGAIN, one might wonder why not just use an image from the RSS feed we get from Google. And once again, I strongly advise against this approach, as it could get you into a lot of trouble.

IMAGES AND PHOTOS used in news posts are the property of the services that publish them. They have either purchased them or created them, and they own the intellectual property rights to use them.

THEREFORE, copying these images would not only be unethical but also violate copyright laws and could expose you (or the company I helped set up the automation for) to financial and reputational damage.

. . .

ALWAYS RESPECT intellectual property rights when preparing or developing automations.

To avoid all these issues, we decided to create our own images. As you probably know, there are many tools available for this. Initially, we planned to use Dall-E, but the quality of the generated photos and images wasn't good enough for us.

ANOTHER POPULAR SOLUTION IS LEONARDO.AI. It's a very good tool and I definitely recommend it for such applications, but we decided to use MidJourney instead.

WITHOUT GETTING into the technical aspects, the whole automation process looks like this:

1. n8n activates at a set time and reads the RSS Feed from Google News.
2. It passes the news to GPT-4, which selects the most relevant topic.
3. The selected topic is then passed to a bot, which uses perplexity to search for more information about it and gather sources.
4. The gathered information is passed to Claude, which uses it to write an article.
5. GPT-4 creates a prompt based on the written article to generate an image.
6. The prompt is sent to MidJourney, which generates the image.

7. All this data is sent to the company's CMS API, which I helped automate, and shortly after, a blog post is created, complete with a hero image, valuable text, and reference links.

This process runs so smoothly and yields such good results that I often find myself reaching for information from the posts it generates (the topics happen to interest me).

We didn't have to wait long for Google to notice these posts. Although the content isn't as unique as when it's generated based on a product feed, the use of multiple sources and a thorough approach still makes it valuable enough and written differently enough that Google started appreciating it and directing some traffic our way.

After about 2-3 months, we noticed that the blog posts generated in this way were being visited by users who found them directly on Google.

7.1.2 Newsletter Approach

Another possible approach to automation is the use of one or several industry newsletters.

For this, it's advisable to set up a new email account, where we can subscribe to a few selected newsletters that cover topics relevant to our industry.

. . .

THEN, we prepare automation similar to the one I described in the previous chapter. However, instead of using an RSS News Feed, we utilize the content from these newsletters. Just like before, we employ a GPT-4 type LLM to identify the most interesting and important topics from the newsletters we receive, which we then explore further through online research.

The rest of the automation process remains the same.

7.3 Practical Sentiment Analysis with Generative AI

Welcome to the exciting world of practical sentiment analysis using generative AI! In this section, we'll dive into the nitty-gritty of how to actually use AI to understand the emotions and opinions hidden in text.

SENTIMENT ANALYSIS IS like teaching a computer to be an emotion detective. It's a powerful tool that can help businesses, researchers, and even everyday people understand how others feel about various topics. With generative AI, we can take this a step further, creating more flexible and powerful sentiment analysis tools.

IN THIS CHAPTER, we'll explore:

1. How to create effective prompts for sentiment analysis
2. The difference between k-shot and zero-shot learning in sentiment analysis
3. Techniques for providing examples to improve AI performance

4. An introduction to prompt engineering specifically for sentiment analysis

Whether you're a business owner wanting to understand customer feedback, a researcher studying public opinion, or just someone curious about AI, this chapter will give you practical skills to start using generative AI for sentiment analysis.

GET ready to unlock the power of AI to read between the lines and understand the emotions behind the words!

THIS INTRODUCTION SETS the stage for a detailed discussion on prompt engineering, k-shot and zero-shot learning, and providing examples in the context of sentiment analysis. You can now proceed to write the detailed content for each of these topics within this section.

WHEN DEALING WITH FULL-SCALE AUTOMATION, especially where dozens of blog posts and social media updates are published daily across various platforms, it's crucial to keep everything in check.

ONE WAY TO monitor and maintain high quality is by using autonomous content critic agents, as mentioned in previous chapters. These 'content critics' ensure the quality of our AI-generated content. If implemented correctly, this should be enough to keep things running smoothly.

. . .

But let's raise the bar and introduce another mechanism to boost the quality of our automation.

When posting on social media, we often have the option to disable comments. While this is one solution, it's not ideal. Social media thrives on interaction and user comments. These interactions improve post visibility and reach. So, blocking comments isn't always the best approach.

However, if we leave comments open, we risk facing problems where users might negatively or unpleasantly react to our brand or product. With a high volume of posts, manually checking comments daily becomes an impossible task.

This is where Generative AI can come to our rescue. Fortunately, there are methods to use it for sentiment analysis. We can easily leverage this to collect all new comments from our social media channels daily and filter them through our generative AI to weed out those with negative sentiment. These comments can be compiled into daily reports, allowing us to take appropriate action.

7.3.1 How to Adapt Generative AI for Sentiment Detection

The best approach is to use the k-shot method combined

with skillful prompt engineering. Here's a practical example below:

This is a text message sentiment classifier

Message: "I can't stand waiting in long lines at the grocery store"

Sentiment: Negative

Message: "Today's weather ruined my plans for a picnic."

Sentiment: Negative

Message: "I'm escatic about the upcoming vacation to Hawaii"

Sentiment: Positive

Message: "Attending the concert last night was a blast!"

Sentiment: Positive

Message: "Finding a parking spot in the city is always a hassle."

Sentiment: Negative

Message: "The sunrise this morning was breathtaking"

Sentiment: Positive

Message: "Dealing with rush hour traffic is frustrating."

Sentiment: Negative

Message: "Receiving flowers unexpectedly made my day"

Sentimet: Positive

Message: "Getting a flat tire on the way to work was so inconvinient."

Sentiment: Negative

Message: "Learning a new language has been challenging but rewarding."

Sentiment:

Positive

USING this method gives us a much higher guarantee that the LLM model will accurately recognize the sentiment of the queries we feed it.

THE PROMPT for sentiment recognition can be modified. Instead of using a single message for recognition, you can provide a list of, say, 10 consecutive messages, and the model should recognize them just as well.

CURRENT MODELS ARE ADVANCED ENOUGH that you can also try a zero-shot approach, which means not providing those 10 examples of sentiment recognition. This should work in some cases.

. . .

However, when we want to fully automate and use this tool on an almost mass scale, it won't be enough for us to have just some cases where it works correctly. We'll want to aim for most, if not all, cases to be correctly recognized. That's exactly what the k-shot method is for. It significantly improves the quality of results and model performance.

In full automation, sentiment recognition is a crucial factor.

Imagine a situation where you've implemented full automation. In a well-executed automation of your SEO content, using the methods or tools I described in the previous chapter, content will appear on your website without your intervention. Completely autonomous AI programs will do all the work for you.

If you want to get the most out of SEO, you'll also integrate your blog with automatic social media posts (as I described).

Since social media is the point of contact between your company and direct user interactions, it's possible that someone might dislike your content, or someone might just enjoy hating on your products, or maybe your competition is playing dirty.

Regardless of the reason, it's worth protecting yourself against such problems and damage to your company's or personal image.

. . .

The ideal solution here would be automation using a single AI agent, prepared to analyze the sentiment of comments under your posts. To do this, you can create a prompt similar to the one I presented here, use it as one of the input parameters for your chosen LLM model, and using tools like N8N, Make, or Zapier, or simply a Python script, prepare a cyclically running automation that will read posts appearing on your social media. Such automation should check new posts daily, examine their sentiment, and record it in a register. You should then prepare weekly and monthly reports showing you the sentiment of your followers.

It's also worth preparing a separate agent to monitor anomalies. This means you'll present it with a "normal" situation using the k-shot method I described, and you'll show it daily reports from the sentiment-analyzing agent so it can recognize anomalies. Such anomalies, whether an unusual increase in positive or negative sentiment, should be reported to you immediately.

9

THINGS TO WATCH OUT FOR

> "The pessimist sees difficulty in every opportunity. The optimist sees opportunity in every difficulty."
>
> **- Winston Churchill**

Welcome to Chapter 8, where we'll explore the potential pitfalls and challenges of using AI in SEO. While AI offers exciting opportunities, it's important to be aware of the risks and how to avoid them.

IN THIS CHAPTER, we'll discuss common mistakes and issues that can arise when implementing AI in your SEO strategy. We'll cover important topics like copyright concerns, the risks of over-relying on AI-generated content, and how to maintain quality and originality in your work.

. . .

We'll also look at some real-world examples of AI implementations gone wrong and learn from these experiences. You'll discover practical tips on how to set up safeguards and checks in your AI processes to prevent errors and ensure your content remains valuable and compliant with search engine guidelines.

Additionally, we'll peek into the future of AI in SEO, discussing emerging trends and best practices that will help you stay ahead of the curve. By the end of this chapter, you'll have a clear understanding of the potential challenges and how to navigate them effectively.

So, let's dive in and learn how to use AI in SEO responsibly and effectively, avoiding the common pitfalls that could hinder your success!

8.1 Copyright laws

As I previously discussed in the section about my real-world implementations, it's crucial to be vigilant about copyright laws.

This is especially true for any images, photos, and other visual elements. It's best to avoid using images from other websites unless they're from stock photo services that offer royalty-free rights. Instead, consider using generative AI to create the necessary images.

This is important whether you're creating content for personal use, your company, or a client. If it turns out that an image is copyrighted and we've used it in an automatically generated blog post, at best, we'll simply have to remove it, losing an eye-catching hero image and wasting time for any posts that featured it. At worst, we might face a fine or legal action.

Moreover, this could lead to reputation damage, especially if we implemented it for a client. Thus, respecting copyright is not only ethically right but also keeps various troubles at bay.

8.2 Critique Agent and the Infinite Loop Issue

Another point of caution is over-reliance on large language models (LLMs). As I've mentioned in previous sections, improper input data or poorly crafted prompts can lead to nonsensical text output. One way to prevent this is to use a system of agents and loop them in the text generation process. You could add an LLM agent whose role would be to critique text generated by another LLM or a different prompt.

The goal of this looped process is to ensure that the resulting text doesn't contain any nonsense and is appropriate to the content and tone we've chosen.

. . .

However, this introduces another risk: the infinite loop. Generative AI, especially LLMs, are designed to provide a response each time they are prompted. If the critic isn't carefully set up to check if the content is correct and to make adjustments only when necessary, it might endlessly make changes. Therefore, this requires careful attention because such automation could not only fail to conclude but also result in substantial costs. This could be a costly mistake, particularly if token limits in the LLM are set relatively high.

8.3 The inadequacy of images - Adding Vision Model

A recent real-life example of issues to watch out for is matching images to blog or social media posts. This is especially important when we're not generating the images ourselves but using them from a Product Feed API.

In our early implementations, we sometimes ran into situations where the image didn't match the description, which created a really unpleasant overall effect.

We solved this by adding another model and validator to our workflow. Alongside our LLM models, we decided to use a Vision model that analyzed images intended for social media posts or as hero images in blog posts. By recognizing what's in the image, the model could generate relevant text, which we then refined using LLM models.

. . .

THIS APPROACH HELPED us avoid problems that can occur when an article based on a product feed covers multiple products.

8.4 Future Outlook and Best Practices

As AI technology evolves, so too must the strategies for its implementation. Staying updated with the latest advancements and regulatory changes is crucial. Businesses should invest in training for their teams not only on how to use these tools effectively but also on understanding their limitations.

BEST PRACTICES WOULD INCLUDE ESTABLISHING a clear AI usage policy, regularly reviewing and updating AI systems in line with technological advancements, and maintaining an ethical approach to AI use. Encouraging openness about the use of AI in creative processes and setting realistic expectations about the outcomes will also play a critical role in integrating these technologies into business operations smoothly and ethically.

BY CAREFULLY MANAGING THESE ASPECTS, companies can harness the full potential of AI to enhance their operations while avoiding the pitfalls that come with technology adoption. This balanced approach will be essential as businesses navigate the increasingly digital and AI-driven landscape.

10

KEY POINTS TO REMEMBER

> "The capacity to learn is a gift; the ability to learn is a skill; the willingness to learn is a choice."
>
> **- Brian Herbert**

Welcome to the final chapter of our journey through AI and SEO! In this chapter, we're going to wrap up everything we've learned and focus on the most important takeaways. Think of it as your quick reference guide for the future.

We'll recap the crucial points about using AI in SEO, highlight the importance of staying up-to-date in this fast-changing field, and offer some practical advice on how to keep your AI-powered SEO strategy on track. We'll also touch on the importance of continuous learning and adaptation in the world of digital marketing.

Whether you're just starting out with AI in SEO or you're looking to refine your existing strategy, this chapter will provide you with a clear set of guidelines to keep in mind. We'll break down complex ideas into simple, actionable steps that you can apply to your own projects.

By the end of this chapter, you'll have a solid understanding of the key principles that will help you navigate the exciting world of AI-powered SEO. So, let's dive in and cement those crucial points that will set you up for success in your digital marketing journey!

Remember that technology, especially the latest advancements, is constantly evolving. AI develops rapidly and changes frequently. Every day, new tools and opportunities emerge.

To stay updated with SEO, it's essential to continually seek new information and check the latest recommendations from search engines.

In cases of full automation, it's also important to periodically verify their operations. You can even set up automations to periodically check all newly created blog posts and report the weakest ones or send alerts when something inappropriate is detected.

In conclusion, I encourage ongoing monitoring and staying informed, as the fields of Generative AI and SEO are incredibly fast-changing.

Expanding on the topic, it's important to highlight the role of continuous learning and adaptation in the technology and SEO sectors. As new algorithms emerge and consumer behavior shifts, staying competitive means staying informed. For instance, Google often updates its search algorithms, which can dramatically affect SEO strategies. Professionals need to adapt quickly to maintain or improve their search engine rankings. This can involve learning new tools or techniques, participating in industry forums, and attending relevant workshops or conferences.

Moreover, the integration of AI into SEO and other areas of digital marketing is no longer a novelty—it's a necessity. AI can analyze data at a scale that's impossible for humans, providing insights that can enhance decision-making processes and optimize marketing strategies. For example, AI can help identify emerging trends or predict changes in consumer behavior, allowing marketers to tailor their strategies more effectively. However, this also means that professionals need to be proficient not only in their core marketing skills but also in understanding and leveraging AI technologies.

Finally, ethical considerations and best practices in using AI and automation in digital marketing cannot be overlooked. As technology becomes more capable of making decisions, ensuring these decisions are fair and do not perpetuate biases is crucial. Transparency in how AI is used, the data it analyzes, and the decisions it influences is essential to maintain trust and comply with regulatory standards. Staying informed about these aspects is just as important as keeping up with technical updates, ensuring that professionals use AI responsibly and effectively in their strategies.

11

CONCLUSION: EMBRACING THE AI REVOLUTION IN SEO

"The future is already here – it's just not evenly distributed."

- William Gibson

As we reach the end of our journey through the world of AI and SEO, it's clear that we're standing at the threshold of a new era in digital marketing. The integration of artificial intelligence into search engine optimization is not just a passing trend, but a fundamental shift that is reshaping how we approach online visibility and content creation.

Let's recap some of the key points we've covered:

AI is transforming SEO by enabling more efficient

content creation, data analysis, and automation of routine tasks.

Google has embraced AI-generated content, provided it meets their quality standards and follows E-E-A-T guidelines.

Various AI tools, from text generators to comprehensive automation solutions, are now available to enhance SEO strategies.

Proper implementation of AI in SEO requires a balance between automation and human oversight to ensure quality and originality.

Ethical considerations and copyright issues are crucial when using AI for content creation.

As we look to the future, it's evident that AI will continue to play an increasingly significant role in SEO. Those who embrace these technologies and learn to use them effectively will have a considerable advantage in the digital landscape.

However, it's important to remember that AI is a tool, not a replacement for human creativity and strategic thinking. The most successful SEO strategies will be those that combine the efficiency and data-processing power of AI with human insight, creativity, and ethical considerations.

Moving Forward

As you implement the strategies and tools discussed in this book, keep these final thoughts in mind:

Stay informed: The field of AI is rapidly evolving. Make it a habit to stay updated on the latest developments and how they might impact SEO.

Experiment and adapt: Don't be afraid to try new AI tools and techniques. What works best for your specific needs may require some trial and error.

Prioritize quality: While AI can help create content more efficiently, never compromise on quality. Your ultimate goal should always be to provide value to your audience.

Be transparent: If you're using AI-generated content, consider being open about it. Transparency can help build trust with your audience.

Keep learning: The integration of AI into SEO is an ongoing process. Commit to continuous learning and improvement.

12

SEO GLOSSARY: KEY TERMS AND CONCEPTS

"The beginning of wisdom is the definition of terms."

— Socrates

Welcome to the SEO Glossary, your go-to reference for understanding the complex world of Search Engine Optimization. As we've explored throughout this book, SEO is a rapidly evolving field, particularly with the advent of AI technologies. The language of SEO can often seem like a maze of technical jargon and industry-specific terms, which can be overwhelming for beginners and even seasoned professionals.

THIS GLOSSARY AIMS to demystify the terminology used in SEO and digital marketing. Whether you're a newcomer trying to grasp the basics or an experienced marketer looking to refresh your knowledge, this comprehensive list of terms will serve as a valuable resource.

We've compiled and simplified definitions for a wide range of SEO concepts, from fundamental principles to advanced techniques. Each entry is explained in clear, concise language, making it easy to understand and apply these concepts to your SEO strategies.

As you navigate through this glossary, you'll find terms related to:

- Technical SEO elements
- On-page and off-page optimization
- Content marketing strategies
- Analytics and performance metrics
- AI and machine learning in SEO
- And much more

Use this glossary as a quick reference when you encounter unfamiliar terms or need a refresher on specific concepts. Remember, understanding the language of SEO is the first step towards mastering its practice.

Let's dive into the world of SEO terminology and equip

ourselves with the knowledge to excel in the ever-changing landscape of digital marketing.

AMP (Accelerated Mobile Pages)

An open-source HTML framework developed by Google to create fast-loading, mobile-optimized web pages.

KEY FEATURES:

- Uses stripped-down HTML, CSS, and JavaScript for improved performance
- Utilizes AMP Cache, a proxy-based CDN for faster content delivery
- Not a direct ranking factor in search engines
- Designed to enhance mobile user experience

AMP pages typically load faster than standard web pages on mobile devices, potentially improving user engagement. However, they can be more challenging to implement and maintain, and may limit some functionality compared to standard web pages. While initially popular, the adoption of AMP has decreased as other mobile optimization techniques have improved.

IMPORTANT NOTE:

Google announced that starting in June 2021, AMP (Accelerated Mobile Pages) will no longer receive preferential treatment in search results, Top Stories carousel, or Google News, as part of their page experience ranking update. This shift removes the requirement for sites to use AMP to rank well, emphasizing instead the importance of fast-loading, user-friendly websites with good Core Web Vitals. The removal of the AMP badge and prioritization of non-AMP content provides more freedom for site owners to choose how they build and optimize their pages. This change also comes amid antitrust scrutiny and criticisms that AMP gave Google excessive control over the web.

Ad Impressions

A digital advertising metric that counts the number of times an advertisement is displayed to users, regardless of user interaction.

Key points:

- Measures ad visibility and reach
- Counted each time an ad loads on a user's screen
- Does not indicate engagement or effectiveness
- Used to calculate other metrics like Click-Through Rate (CTR)
- Important for brand awareness campaigns

Ad impressions provide insight into how often an advertisement is seen, but should be considered alongside other metrics like clicks, conversions, and engagement rates for a comprehensive understanding of ad performance. This metric is particularly relevant for CPM (Cost Per Mille) pricing models in digital advertising.

. . .

ADA Website Compliance

The practice of designing and developing websites to be accessible to users with disabilities, in accordance with the Americans with Disabilities Act (ADA).

Key aspects include:

- Screen reader compatibility
- Keyboard navigation
- Clear and consistent layout
- Text alternatives for non-text content
- Closed captioning and transcripts
- Adjustable text size and color contrast
- Error identification and instructions

While not directly influencing SEO, ADA compliance often aligns with SEO best practices, potentially improving site structure, usability, and content accessibility. Compliance helps avoid legal issues and ensures equal access for all users, regardless of disability. It's typically guided by Web Content Accessibility Guidelines (WCAG) standards.

Alt Text

A descriptive text attribute added to image HTML tags to provide a textual alternative for visual content.

. . .

Key points:

- Syntax: alt="Description of image"
- Primary purpose: Improve accessibility for visually impaired users

SEO benefits:

- Helps search engines understand image content

Best practices:

1. Be descriptive and concise (under 100 characters)
2. Include relevant keywords naturally, avoid keyword stuffing
3. Focus on informative images, not decorative ones
4. Audit website for missing alt texts

Alt text is crucial for web accessibility, allowing screen readers to convey image content to visually impaired users. It also supports SEO efforts by providing context to search engines, potentially improving image search rankings and overall page relevance. Well-crafted alt text balances descriptive accuracy with SEO considerations.

Anchor Text

The clickable text in a hyperlink that provides context about the linked page or resource.

Key points:

- Types include: exact match, phrase match, partial match, branded, generic, image alt text, and naked URL
- Important for both user experience and SEO
- Helps search engines understand the content of the linked page

Best practices:

1. Make sense without surrounding context
2. Avoid keyword stuffing
3. Diversify anchor text variations

ANCHOR TEXT PLAYS a crucial role in conveying information to users and search engines about the destination of a link. While it's considered a ranking factor, overoptimization should be avoided. For image links, the alt text serves as the anchor text. Proper use of anchor text can improve user navigation and potentially influence search engine rankings.

BACKLINKS

Incoming links from one webpage to another, also known as inbound links.

KEY POINTS:

- Serve as "votes of confidence" from one site to another

- Major ranking factor for search engines
- Quality, quantity, relevance, and authority of backlinks matter
- Anchor text of backlinks provides context for linked content
- Building high-quality backlinks is a core SEO strategy (link building)

Backlinks are crucial for SEO as they signal to search engines that others vouch for your content. The more high-quality, relevant backlinks a page has, the more likely it is to rank well in search results. However, quality is more important than quantity, and artificially manipulating backlinks can lead to penalties. Effective backlink strategies focus on creating valuable content that naturally attracts links from authoritative sources.

BWT (Bing Webmaster Tools)

A free suite of tools provided by Microsoft's Bing search engine to help webmasters manage and optimize their websites' performance in Bing search results.

Key features include:

- Sitemap submission
- URL indexing control
- Backlinks report
- Keyword research tool
- Site audit functionality

- Search performance analytics

While primarily designed for Bing, these tools can also benefit overall SEO efforts, including Google optimization. Bing Webmaster Tools offers insights into how Bing crawls and indexes websites, helping webmasters identify and resolve issues that may affect search visibility. It's a valuable resource for comprehensive search engine optimization strategies, especially for markets where Bing has a significant market share.

Black Hat SEO

Unethical search engine optimization practices that violate search engine guidelines to manipulate rankings.

Key aspects:

- Aims for short-term gains at the risk of penalties
- Violates search engine policies

Common tactics include:

- Buying links
- Using private blog networks (PBNs)
- Generating low-quality automated content
- Negative SEO against competitors
- Creating unnatural link patterns

While potentially effective short-term, black hat SEO risks severe penalties, including manual actions or algorithmic devaluations. It contrasts with white hat SEO, which focuses on ethical, user-centric practices. Grey hat SEO blends both approaches. While not illegal, some black hat tactics may cross into unlawful activities. Search engines continually improve detection of these practices, making them increasingly risky and unsustainable for long-term SEO success.

Bounce Rate

The percentage of visitors who leave a website after viewing only one page, without further interaction.

Key points:

- Calculated as: (Single-page visits / Total visits) x 100
- Measures initial user engagement and content relevance
- Lower bounce rates generally indicate better user experience

Factors affecting bounce rate:
- Website design and usability
- Content quality and relevance
- Page load speed
- Mobile optimization
- Traffic source quality

Improving bounce rate involves enhancing user experience, creating engaging content, optimizing for mobile, improving site speed, and attracting qualified traffic. While a lower bounce rate is generally desirable, interpretation varies by industry and page type. For instance, informational pages might naturally have higher bounce rates than e-commerce pages. Regular analysis and adjustment of high-bounce pages can lead to overall site improvement and better user engagement.

Breadcrumb Navigation

A secondary navigation scheme that shows users their current location within a website's hierarchy.

Key points:

- Typically displayed as a horizontal line of links near the top of a page
- Named after the trail of breadcrumbs in the Hansel and Gretel fairy tale

Types:

- Hierarchy-based (most common)
- Attribute-based (common in e-commerce)
- History-based (shows user's path)

Benefits:

- Improves user experience and site navigation

- Enhances SEO by clarifying site structure
- Can appear in search results, improving click-through rates
- May reduce bounce rates by encouraging further exploration

BEST PRACTICES:

1. Use as a supplement to main navigation, not a replacement
2. Separate links with characters like ">" or "/"
3. Read left to right, from highest to lowest level
4. Keep design simple and unobtrusive

BREADCRUMB NAVIGATION IS PARTICULARLY useful for large, multi-level websites, helping users understand their location and easily navigate to higher-level pages.

BROKEN Link

A hyperlink that points to a non-existent web page or resource, typically resulting in a 404 (Not Found) or 410 (Gone) error.

KEY POINTS:

Types:

- Broken outgoing links: from your site to non-existent pages
- Broken backlinks: from other sites to non-existent pages on your site

IMPACT:

- Can negatively affect user experience
- Wastes crawl budget for search engines
- Broken backlinks represent lost link equity opportunities

DETECTION:

- SEO tools like ScreamingFrog, Ahrefs Site Explorer or Webmaster Tools
- Regular site audits and crawls

FIXING:

- For outgoing links: replace, remove, or redirect
- For broken backlinks: recreate content, redirect, or reach out to linking sites

While some broken links are normal, excessive numbers can harm SEO and user experience. Regular monitoring and fixing of broken links is an important aspect of website maintenance and SEO strategy.

Cached Page

A stored copy of a web page or resource, saved to improve retrieval speed and performance.

Key points:

Types of caching:

- Browser caching: Stores local copies for faster reloading
- Server caching: CDNs store copies closer to users
- Search engine caching: Backup copies for when live pages are unavailable

Benefits:

- Faster page load times
- Reduced bandwidth usage and server load
- Improved user experience
- Backup access when original pages are down

Search engine caching:

- Google stores snapshots of crawled pages
- Cached versions viewable from search results
- Can be disabled using “noarchive” meta tag

Caching is crucial for web performance optimization, allowing faster content delivery and providing fallback options when original pages are inaccessible. While generally beneficial, webmasters can control caching behavior to manage content freshness and privacy concerns.

Canonical Tag

An HTML element that specifies the preferred version of a web page when multiple similar or duplicate pages exist.

Key points:

- Syntax:

```
<link rel="canonical" href="https://example.com/preferred-page">
```

- Helps search engines identify the main version of content to index
- Consolidates link signals from duplicate pages to the canonical version
- Best practices:

- Use self-referential canonical tags
- Use absolute URLs
- Don't rely on robots.txt for canonicalization
- Regularly audit for proper implementation

WHILE NOT MANDATORY, canonical tags are crucial for managing duplicate content issues and ensuring the correct page version is indexed and ranked in search results. They help prevent dilution of SEO value across similar pages and provide clear direction to search engines about your preferred content.

CANONICAL URL

The preferred version of a web page when multiple similar or duplicate versions exist.

KEY POINTS:

- Helps search engines identify the primary version to index
- Implemented using the canonical tag in HTML:

<link rel="canonical" href="https://example.com/canonical-page/" />

- Important for managing duplicate content issues

Best practices:

1. Use self-referencing canonical tags
2. Exclude non-canonical URLs from sitemaps
3. Avoid setting 404 pages as canonical
4. Use absolute URLs in canonical tags

Canonical URLs are crucial for SEO, helping to consolidate ranking signals to the preferred page version and preventing issues with duplicate content. While Google may choose a different canonical URL, properly implementing canonical tags provides a strong signal for your preferred version. Regular auditing of canonical implementation is recommended to ensure optimal search engine understanding of your site structure.

Cloaking

A deceptive SEO technique that presents different content or URLs to search engines and human users.

Key points:

- Violates search engine guidelines
- Considered a black-hat SEO tactic

Methods:

- IP-based detection of search engine bots
- User-agent manipulation

- JavaScript-based content switching

RISKS:

- Severe search engine penalties
- Potential de-indexing of website
- Loss of credibility and organic traffic

DETECTION:

- Comparing cached pages with live content
- Using tools like Google Search Console
- Analyzing discrepancies between bot and user views

CLOAKING undermines search engine integrity and user experience. While it may temporarily boost rankings, the long-term risks far outweigh any short-term benefits. Search engines actively combat cloaking, and engaging in this practice can result in significant damage to a website's visibility and reputation.

CDN (CONTENT DELIVERY Network)

A geographically distributed network of servers that work together to deliver web content faster by reducing the physical distance between the website's origin server and the end user.

Key aspects include:

- Uses edge servers to cache and serve content from locations closer to users
- Improves website load times and user experience
- Assists with load balancing during traffic surges
- Enhances website availability and uptime
- Provides additional security against certain cyber threats (e.g., DDoS attacks)

While CDNs don't directly impact SEO rankings, they can indirectly benefit SEO by improving site speed and user experience, which are factors in search engine algorithms. Major CDN providers include Cloudflare, Akamai, and Amazon CloudFront.

Worth noting:

In the context of CDNs, it's important to highlight that new frameworks for building websites, like JAMstack, can often be fully distributed through a CDN. This significantly improves their load speed, so it's worth getting familiar with static websites and JAMstack as great solutions for SEO. My favorite framework for static sites is AstroJS. Other popular ones include GatsbyJS, 11ty, and Hugo. Frameworks that partially support static content include NextJS and NuxtJS.

Content Gap Analysis

A strategic process in content marketing and SEO to

identify topics or areas not adequately covered on a website compared to competitors.

Key points:

Purpose:

- Uncover missed content opportunities

Process:

- Compare your content with competitors'
- Identify topics you're not addressing
- Analyze audience needs and interests

Benefits:

- Improved content strategy
- Enhanced search engine rankings
- Increased website traffic and relevance
- Better audience engagement

Tools:

- SEO software (e.g., Ahrefs Site Explorer, SEMRush, ScreamingFrog)
- Keyword research tools
- Competitor analysis platforms

Content gap analysis helps create a more comprehensive content strategy by identifying areas where competitors may be outperforming you. It's not about copying competitors, but understanding market demands and filling gaps in your own content. This approach can lead to a more authoritative online presence and better alignment with audience needs.

Content Relevance

The degree to which content aligns with the needs, interests, and preferences of its target audience.

Key factors:

- Audience understanding
- Keyword research
- Timeliness
- Personalization
- Contextual appropriateness

Importance:

- Increases user engagement
- Builds trust and authority
- Improves conversion rates
- Enhances search engine rankings

Content relevance is crucial for effective content marketing and SEO. It ensures that content resonates with the intended audience, addressing their specific needs and search intents. Relevant content is more likely to attract and retain users, establish the brand as a thought leader, and drive desired actions. Search engines also prioritize relevant content, making it a key factor in improving visibility in search results.

Core Web Vitals

A set of specific factors that Google considers important in a webpage's overall user experience. These metrics are part of Google's Page Experience signals used in ranking web pages.

The five Core Web Vitals are:

1. First Contentful Paint (FCP): Measures the time from when the user first navigated to the page to when any part of the page's content is rendered on the screen
2. Largest Contentful Paint (LCP): Measures loading performance
3. Total Blocking Time (TBT): Measures interactivity
4. Cumulative Layout Shift (CLS): Measures visual stability
5. Speed Index (SI): Measures how quickly content is visually displayed during page load.

Importance:

- Directly impacts search engine rankings
- Improves user experience
- Enhances website performance

Core Web Vitals provide a standardized way to measure and improve key aspects of user experience on the web. By optimizing these metrics, website owners can potentially improve their search rankings and provide a better experience for their users. Google provides tools like PageSpeed Insights and Search Console to help measure and monitor these vitals.

Crawl Budget

The number of pages a search engine can and wants to crawl on a website within a specific timeframe.

Key points:

Determined by:

- Crawl demand: Based on page count, update frequency, and popularity
- Crawl rate limit: Influenced by server capabilities and crawl settings

Importance:

- Affects how many pages search engines crawl and index
- Crucial for large websites or those with frequent content changes

Optimization strategies:

- Improve server speed and page load times
- Increase internal and external linking
- Fix broken links and minimize redirects
- Use Indexing API when applicable

Monitoring:

- Check Crawl Stats report in Google Search Console

Crawl budget is primarily a concern for very large websites (1M+ pages) or those with frequent content updates. For most smaller sites, it's not a significant issue. Optimizing crawl budget ensures search engines efficiently crawl and index your most important pages, potentially improving overall site visibility in search results.

Crawlability

The ability of search engine bots to access and navigate through a website's pages and resources.

Key points:

- Distinct from indexability (ability to be added to search index)
- Crucial for organic search visibility

Factors affecting crawlability:

- Page discoverability (sitemaps, internal linking)
- Nofollow links
- Robots.txt directives
- Access restrictions (login requirements, IP blocking)

Importance:

- Enables search engines to read and analyze content
- Essential for proper indexing and ranking

Detection:

- Use SEO tools like Ahrefs Site Audit or Webmaster Tools

CRAWLABILITY IS fundamental for SEO success. Without it, pages may not be discovered or properly indexed by search engines, regardless of content quality. Regularly monitoring and addressing crawlability issues ensures that search engines can efficiently access and understand your website's content, potentially improving search visibility and rankings.

CRAWLER

An automated program designed to systematically browse and analyze web pages. Also known as web spiders or bots.

KEY POINTS:

TYPES:

- Constant-crawling (e.g., Googlebot)
- On-demand (e.g., AhrefsSiteAudit bot)

FUNCTIONS:

- Discover and index web pages for search engines

- Analyze website structure and content
- Gather data for SEO audits

Importance:

- Essential for search engine indexing and ranking
- Enables website analysis and optimization

💡 Best practices for crawler-friendly websites:

1. Optimize robots.txt file
2. Submit sitemaps
3. Use crawler directives wisely
4. Implement effective internal linking
5. Minimize errors and unnecessary redirects
6. Regularly audit for crawlability issues

Crawlers are fundamental to how search engines operate and how websites are discovered online. Understanding and optimizing for crawlers is crucial for ensuring a website's visibility in search results and overall SEO performance.

Customer Journey

The complete sequence of interactions and experiences a customer has with a brand, from initial awareness to post-purchase engagement. In SEO context:

Stages:
1. Awareness: Recognition of need or problem
SEO focus: Educational content, broad keywords
2. Consideration: Evaluation of options
SEO focus: Comparative content, specific keywords
3. Decision: Ready to purchase
SEO focus: Product pages, high-intent keywords
4. Post-purchase: Satisfaction and loyalty
SEO focus: Support content, related product information

IMPORTANCE FOR SEO:

- Aligns content with customer needs at each stage
- Guides keyword strategy and content creation
- Enhances user experience and engagement
- Improves conversion rates and customer retention

THE CUSTOMER JOURNEY concept helps create a more targeted and effective SEO strategy, ensuring that the right content reaches the right audience at the right time in their decision-making process. It requires ongoing refinement to match evolving customer behaviors and search trends.

DOFOLLOW LINK

A hyperlink without "nofollow," "UGC," or "sponsored" attributes, allowing search engine crawlers to follow and pass link equity. Key points:

. . .

HTML syntax:

<a href="https://example.com">Anchor text</a>

Importance:

- Helps search engines discover content
- Passes link equity, influencing search rankings
- Essential for effective backlink strategies

Identification methods:

- Inspect page source code
- Use browser extensions like Ahrefs SEO Toolbar

Analysis:

- Use SEO tools (e.g., Ahrefs Site Explorer) to identify dofollow backlinks

Dofollow links are crucial for SEO as they contribute to a website's authority and search engine rankings. Unlike nofollow links, which only provide referral traffic, dofollow links pass both traffic and link equity. Understanding and acquiring quality dofollow links is a key aspect of successful link-building strategies and overall SEO efforts.

Domain Structure

The hierarchical organization of a website's domain name, subdomains, and directories.

. . .

Key components:

1. Root domain: Main website address (e.g., example.com)
2. Subdomains: Extensions of root domain (e.g., blog.example.com)
3. Directories/paths: Content organization after domain (e.g., example.com/products)

Importance:

- SEO: Helps search engines understand and index content
- User Experience: Facilitates intuitive navigation
- Website Management: Simplifies content organization and updates
- Branding: Enables strategic segmentation of content areas

Best practices:

1. Keep structure logical and intuitive
2. Use descriptive, keyword-rich URLs
3. Limit subdomain use unless necessary
4. Maintain consistent structure across the site

A WELL-PLANNED domain structure enhances both SEO performance and user experience. It provides clear signals to search engines about content hierarchy and relevance, while also making it easier for users to navigate and find information. Proper domain structuring is a fundamental aspect of effective website architecture and content organization.

Duplicate Content

Identical or very similar content appearing at more than one URL, either on the same website or across different websites. Key points:

Types:

- Exact duplicates: Identical content at different URLs
- Near-duplicates: Very similar content with minor differences

SEO Impact:

- Not directly penalized by Google (unless intentionally manipulative)
- Can lead to undesired URLs in search results
- May dilute link equity
- Can waste crawl budget

COMMON CAUSES:

- URL parameters (e.g., tracking, session IDs)
- WWW vs. non-WWW versions
- HTTP vs. HTTPS
- Faceted navigation
- Pagination
- Print/mobile-friendly versions

SOLUTIONS:

- Use canonical tags
- Implement proper redirects
- Use robots.txt or meta robots tags
- Consolidate similar content
- Proper implementation of hreflang for localized content

DETECTION:

- Use SEO tools like, ScreamingFrog, Ahrefs Site Audit, SEMRush
- Check Google Search Console for warnings
- Use tools like Copyscape for cross-site duplication

WHILE NOT ALWAYS HARMFUL, managing duplicate content is important for maintaining SEO effectiveness and ensuring the most valuable version of content is indexed and ranked.

DWELL TIME

The amount of time a user spends on a webpage after clicking through from search engine results before returning to the search results page.

KEY POINTS:

- Not the same as bounce rate or time on page
- Theorized to be a potential search engine ranking factor
- Not officially confirmed by Google as a ranking signal
- No way to directly measure or calculate dwell time

IMPORTANCE:

- May indicate user satisfaction with search results
- Potentially influences search engine rankings
- Encourages focus on user engagement and content quality

Best practices to potentially improve dwell time:

1. Create engaging introductions
2. Match search intent
3. Avoid clickbait titles and descriptions
4. Cover relevant subtopics
5. Keep content up-to-date
6. Use internal linking effectively

While not directly measurable, focusing on improving dwell time can lead to better overall user experience and potentially improved search engine performance. It's part of a broader strategy to create engaging, valuable content that satisfies user needs.

Dynamic URL

A web address that is generated on-the-fly and typically includes parameters to pull specific content from a database.

Key characteristics:

- Contains characters like ?, =, &
- Often used in e-commerce and database-driven websites
- Example: https://example.com/products?category=shoes&color=red

Importance:

- Enables customized content display based on user input
- Allows for efficient management of large, database-driven websites

SEO Considerations:

- Less readable than static URLs
- Potential for duplicate content issues
- May impact click-through rates in search results

Best Practices:

1. Use canonical tags to prevent duplicate content
2. Keep URLs as short as possible
3. Consider user-friendly URL structures when feasible

While dynamic URLs are crucial for many websites, especially those with large databases, they require careful management to ensure optimal SEO performance. Modern search engines can effectively crawl and index dynamic URLs, so converting them to static URLs is generally unnecessary unless there are specific user experience or technical concerns.

. . .

Ego Bait

A content marketing tactic that involves creating content designed to appeal to the ego of influential individuals or brands, with the goal of gaining backlinks, shares, or engagement.

Key points:

Types:

- Expert roundups
- Top lists or awards
- Interviews
- Mentions and acknowledgements
- Collaborative content

Benefits:

- Builds relationships with influencers
- Increases content visibility and reach
- Potentially improves SEO through high-quality backlinks

Best practices:

1. Choose appropriate targets
2. Provide genuine value
3. Personalize content
4. Focus on quality over quantity

5. Follow up politely
6. Use authentically and sparingly
7. Monitor and analyze results

Ego bait, when used effectively, can be a powerful tool for expanding reach, building industry relationships, and improving SEO. However, it should be implemented thoughtfully and ethically, balancing flattery with genuine value to maintain credibility and effectiveness.

Entity-Based SEO

An advanced SEO approach that focuses on optimizing for entities (unique, well-defined concepts) rather than just keywords.

Key aspects:

- Entities: People, places, things, or concepts
- Focus: Context and relationships between entities
- Goal: Align with search engines' understanding of semantic search

Key strategies:

1. Entity identification in content
2. Establishing contextual relevance
3. Implementing structured data (schema markup)
4. Building topical authority

Importance:

- Aligns with modern search engine algorithms
- Improves content relevance and search accuracy
- Enhances understanding of user intent
- Supports more natural language processing in search

Entity-based SEO represents a shift from traditional keyword-centric optimization to a more holistic approach that considers the meanings and relationships behind words. This method aims to create content that better matches user intent and search engine understanding, potentially leading to improved search visibility and user engagement.

Entry Page

The first page a visitor lands on when accessing a website, regardless of whether it's the homepage or any other page.

Key points:

- Can be any page on the site
- Often referred to as "Landing Page" in Google Analytics
- Different from marketing-specific landing pages

Importance:

- Forms first impressions of website design and quality
- Influences user engagement and bounce rates

- Key to guiding visitors to conversion-focused pages

Optimization strategies:

- Ensure fast loading speeds
- Provide excellent user experience
- Include clear navigation to key pages
- Optimize for mobile devices
- Include relevant internal links

Analysis:

- Use analytics tools to identify most common entry pages
- Monitor metrics like bounce rate and time on page
- Continuously improve based on user behavior data

Entry pages play a crucial role in user experience and website performance. Optimizing these pages can significantly impact overall site engagement, conversions, and search engine rankings. Regular analysis and improvement of entry pages is an important aspect of effective SEO and digital marketing strategies.

Evergreen Content

Search-optimized content that remains relevant and valuable over an extended period, often generating consistent traffic long after publication.

. . .

Key characteristics:

- Topics with enduring interest (e.g., "How to tie a tie")
- Not tied to specific dates, seasons, or trends
- Consistently attracts organic search traffic

Importance:

- Provides steady, long-term traffic
- Builds authority in a niche
- Offers high ROI for content creation efforts

Creation strategies:

- Research topics with steady search trends
- Analyze competitors' consistently high-traffic pages
- Create comprehensive, high-quality content (10x content)
- Optimize for search engines

Maintenance:

- Regular updates to keep information current
- Monitor rankings and traffic
- Ongoing link-building efforts

Evergreen content forms a cornerstone of effective content marketing and SEO strategies. While it requires significant initial investment and ongoing maintenance, it can provide long-lasting value, attracting consistent traffic and establishing topical authority. The key to success with evergreen content lies in choosing the right topics, creating superior content, and maintaining its relevance over time.

External Link

A hyperlink on a website that directs users to a page or resource on a different domain. Also known as outbound links.

Key points:

- Connects different websites
- Opposite of internal links (links within the same domain)
- Important for user experience and information flow

SEO Importance:

- May contribute to a site's perceived authority
- Helps search engines understand content context
- Counted as backlinks for the linked site

Best Practices:

1. Link to reputable, relevant sources
2. Use descriptive anchor text
3. Avoid excessive linking or link schemes
4. Consider using "nofollow" or "sponsored" attributes when appropriate
5. Regularly audit external links for broken or redirected URLs

Considerations:

- Balance between providing value and retaining "link juice"
- Potential SEO impact (positive or negative)
- User experience and content credibility

External links play a crucial role in the web's interconnectedness and can enhance content value and user experience when used properly. While they can support SEO efforts, it's important to use them judiciously and in accordance with search engine guidelines to avoid potential penalties.

Faceted Navigation

A user interface element that allows users to filter and sort large sets of content or products based on multiple criteria simultaneously.

Key points:

- Common on e-commerce, job boards, and content-rich sites
- Enhances user experience by simplifying content discovery
- Can create SEO challenges if not properly implemented

Pros:

- Improves user experience

- Facilitates quick and precise content filtering
- Accommodates complex search needs

SEO Challenges:

- Can create duplicate content issues
- May waste crawl budget
- Potential for keyword cannibalization

Best Practices:

1. Use canonical tags to manage duplicate content
2. Implement proper URL structure
3. Utilize robots meta tags or robots.txt to control crawling
4. Consider AJAX for dynamic loading without changing URLs
5. Prioritize indexing of valuable combination pages

Faceted navigation, when implemented correctly, can significantly enhance user experience and site usability. However, it requires careful SEO consideration to avoid potential issues with search engine crawling, indexing, and ranking. Balancing user needs with search engine optimization is key to successful implementation.

Gated Content

Digital content that requires users to provide information or payment before accessing.

. . .

KEY POINTS:

TYPES:

- Lead magnets (e.g., downloadable guides, webinars)
- Paywalled articles (e.g., subscription-based news sites)

PURPOSE:

- Lead generation
- Monetization

SEO CHALLENGES:

- Difficult for search engines to crawl and index
- May be misinterpreted as cloaking

Strategies for SEO:

- Provide content summaries
- Implement Flexible Sampling
- Use structured data to indicate gated content
- Apply "noarchive" meta tags

Pros:

- Generates qualified leads
- Creates perceived value

Cons:

- Limits content visibility
- May reduce organic search traffic

Gated content is a powerful tool for lead generation and monetization but requires careful implementation to balance user access with SEO performance. Effective use involves strategic decisions about what content to gate and how to make it discoverable to search engines while maintaining its exclusive nature.

Gateway Page (Doorway Page)

A web page designed primarily to rank for specific search queries without providing valuable content, often redirecting visitors to another page.

Key points:

- Purpose: To manipulate search engine rankings
- Considered a black-hat SEO technique
- Violates Google's quality guidelines

Characteristics:

- Keyword-stuffed content
- Little to no valuable information
- Often uses redirects or cloaking techniques

Risks:

- Potential for manual penalties from search engines
- Poor user experience
- Decreased site credibility

Alternatives:

- Create high-quality pages targeting multiple relevant keywords
- Focus on long-tail keywords with legitimate content
- Use proper server-side redirects when necessary

Gateway pages are strongly discouraged in SEO as they prioritize search engine manipulation over user value. Instead, focus on creating content that genuinely serves user needs while following search engine guidelines. This approach leads to better long-term SEO results and improved user satisfaction.

Google Alerts (https://www.google.com/alerts)

A free Google service that monitors the web for new content matching specific search queries and sends email notifications to users.

Key features:

- Customizable search queries
- Adjustable notification frequency

- Supports advanced search operators

Uses:

1. Brand monitoring
2. Competitor analysis
3. Content discovery
4. Link building opportunities

SEO Applications:

- Finding unlinked brand mentions
- Discovering guest posting opportunities
- Monitoring for link injection hacks
- Identifying industry trends and discussions

Best Practices:

1. Use specific, targeted queries
2. Utilize advanced search operators for precision
3. Adjust frequency based on query importance
4. Combine with other monitoring tools for comprehensive coverage

Google Alerts is a versatile tool for staying informed about specific topics, brands, or competitors. While useful for basic monitoring, it may have limitations in comprehensiveness compared to specialized SEO tools. For more thorough web monitoring, consider using Google Alerts in conjunction with professional SEO software.

Google Algorithm

A complex system of instructions and processes used by Google to retrieve, analyze, and rank content from its search index based on user queries.

Key points:

- Comprises multiple sub-algorithms
- Constantly updated and refined
- Major changes announced as "core updates"

Key Components:

- Core Algorithm: The main search algorithm
- Ranking Algorithm: Determines page order in search results
- PageRank: Assesses page importance based on links
- Spam Algorithm: Identifies and penalizes policy violations
- RankBrain: Machine learning for query interpretation

Significance:

- Determines search result relevance and quality
- Impacts website visibility and traffic
- Influences SEO strategies

IMPORTANT UPDATES:

- Panda (February 24, 2011): *Focused on content quality. It lowered the rankings of websites with low-quality content, duplicates, or too many ads.*
- Penguin (April 24, 2012): *Targeted unnatural links and link manipulation tactics, such as excessive use of keywords in backlinks.*
- Hummingbird (August 22, 2013): *Improved the understanding of context and user intent, allowing for more accurate results for complex queries.*
- Pigeon (July 24, 2014): *Enhanced local search results by more closely integrating them with traditional ranking factors.*
- Mobile-Friendly Update (Mobilegeddon) (April 21, 2015): *Gave preference to mobile-optimized sites in mobile search results.*
- RankBrain (October 26, 2015): *Introduced AI and machine learning to better interpret user queries.*
- Possum (September 1, 2016): *Increased diversity in local search results by filtering out duplicate content and factoring in the user's location.*
- Fred (March 7, 2017): *Targeted low-quality sites focused on profit at the expense of user value, often with excessive ads.*
- Medic Update (August 1, 2018): *Significantly impacted health and medical websites, with a focus on content authority and trustworthiness.*
- BERT (October 25, 2019): *Improved the algorithm's understanding of natural language, allowing better interpretation of context in queries.*
- Core Updates (Various dates, e.g., March 2019, June 2019, January 2020): *General algorithm*

updates affecting rankings across a wide range of sites, without specific guidance on the changes.

- Page Experience Update (June 2021): *Introduced Core Web Vitals as ranking factors, emphasizing user experience on websites.*
- Product Reviews Update (April 2021, December 2021): *Promoted high-quality, in-depth product reviews, rewarding sites offering detailed analysis.*
- Spam Updates (June 2021, November 2021): *Updates aimed at combating spam in search results by removing sites that violate Google's guidelines.*
- Link Spam Update (July 2021): *Targeted unnatural links and spamming practices related to link building.*
- Helpful Content Update (August 2022): *Aimed to promote content that provides real value to users while lowering the rankings of sites with low-quality content.*
- March 2023 Core Update (March 2023): *Another broad algorithm update affecting a wide range of sites, with an emphasis on content quality.*
- April 2023 Reviews Update (April 2023): *Expanded previous review updates to include not only product reviews but also reviews of other services and goods.*
- August 2024 Core Update: *Useful content update.*

UNDERSTANDING GOOGLE'S algorithm and its updates is crucial for SEO professionals and webmasters. While the full workings are not public, Google provides guidelines for creating high-quality, user-focused content that aligns with their algorithmic preferences.

. . .

GA (Google Analytics)

A free web analytics service provided by Google that tracks and reports website traffic. Key features:

- Tracks user behavior and interactions
- Provides detailed traffic data and sources
- Offers insights on user demographics and interests
- Measures website performance and conversions

Key Components:

- Acquisition: How users find your website
- Engagement: User interactions on your site
- Conversions: Goal completions and e-commerce data

Important Concepts:

- Metrics: Quantitative measurements (e.g., sessions, bounce rate)
- Dimensions: Attributes of data (e.g., source, medium, location)

SEO Applications:

- Identifying high-performing content
- Discovering keyword opportunities through internal search
- Analyzing organic traffic patterns
- Evaluating landing page performance

Best Practices:

1. Regular monitoring of key metrics
2. Setting up goals and conversions
3. Utilizing custom reports for specific insights
4. Integrating with other Google tools (e.g., Search Console)

Google Analytics is an essential tool for understanding website performance and user behavior. It provides valuable data for SEO strategy, content optimization, and overall digital marketing efforts. Proper setup and interpretation of Google Analytics data can significantly improve website effectiveness and user experience.

Google Autocomplete

A search feature that predicts and displays possible search queries as users type in the Google search box.

Key points:

- Based on real searches by other users and personal search history
- Aims to complete intended searches, not suggest new ones
- Available on Google homepage, mobile app, and Chrome address bar

Importance for SEO:

- Provides insight into popular and trending search queries
- Useful for keyword research and content ideation

- Reflects user intent and search behavior

Content Filtering:

- Removes sexually explicit, hateful, violent, or dangerous predictions
- Users can report inappropriate predictions

SEO Applications:

- Keyword research tool for identifying related search terms
- Understanding user search patterns and intents
- Informing content strategy and topic selection

Best Practices:

1. Use for initial keyword ideation
2. Combine with other keyword research tools for comprehensive analysis
3. Consider regional variations in predictions

Google Autocomplete offers valuable insights into user search behavior and can be a useful tool for SEO professionals in keyword research and content planning. However, it should be used in conjunction with other SEO tools for a more comprehensive keyword strategy.

Google Bombing

An attempt to manipulate search engine results by creating numerous backlinks with specific anchor text to a target webpage, often for humorous or political purposes.

. . .

KEY POINTS:

- Exploits search engine reliance on backlinks and anchor text
- Often aims to rank unrelated content for specific search queries
- Peaked in popularity in the early 2000s

Historical Significance:

- Demonstrated vulnerabilities in early search algorithms
- Led to improvements in Google's ranking algorithms

Notable Examples:

- "More evil than Satan himself" → Microsoft homepage (1999)
- "Miserable failure" → George W. Bush's biography (2003)

Google's Response:

- Implemented "Google Bomb Fix" in 2007
- Continually updates algorithms to minimize such manipulations

SEO Implications:

- Highlights the importance of anchor text in link building
- Emphasizes the need for relevant, natural anchor text
- Underscores Google's efforts to combat search manipulation

While Google Bombing is less effective today due to algorithm improvements, it remains a part of search engine history and illustrates the ongoing challenge of balancing link signals with content relevance in search rankings.

Google Business Profile

A free tool provided by Google that allows businesses to manage their online presence across Google Search and Maps.

Key features:

- Displays business information in local search results
- Appears on Google Maps
- Allows businesses to manage reviews and customer interactions

Components:

- Business name, address, and phone number (NAP)
- Operating hours
- Photos and videos

- Products and services
- Customer reviews and ratings

Importance for SEO:

- Critical for local SEO strategies
- Improves visibility in local search results
- Enhances credibility and trust with potential customers

Best Practices:

1. Provide accurate and complete information
2. Regularly update business details
3. Respond to customer reviews
4. Add high-quality photos and videos
5. Use Posts feature for updates and promotions

Setup Process:

- Create profile at Google Business Profile website
- Verify business ownership (usually via mail, phone, or email)
- Optimize profile with comprehensive information

Google Business Profile is an essential tool for local businesses to improve their online visibility and engage with customers. It plays a crucial role in local SEO efforts and can significantly impact a business's local search rankings and customer interactions.

. . .

Google Dance

A term in SEO referring to temporary fluctuations in search engine rankings, particularly on Google.

Key aspects:

- Causes:
- New websites or pages being indexed
- Google algorithm updates
- Temporary technical issues
- Historical context:
- Originally referred to monthly index updates (pre-2003)
- Also referred to Google-organized events for web professionals

Significance for SEO:

- Indicates Google's ongoing evaluation of web content
- Can affect short-term search visibility and traffic
- Often precedes more permanent ranking changes

Best practices:

1. Monitor rankings regularly
2. Avoid overreacting to short-term fluctuations
3. Focus on long-term SEO strategies
4. Stay informed about Google algorithm updates

While potentially concerning for website owners,

Google Dance is a normal part of search engine behavior. It underscores the dynamic nature of search rankings and the importance of maintaining consistent, high-quality SEO practices rather than reacting to every fluctuation.

Google Knowledge Graph

A database of facts about entities (people, places, things) and their relationships, used by Google to enhance search results with contextual information.

Key aspects:

- Powers Knowledge Panels in search results
- Focuses on entities rather than keywords
- Draws data from sources like Wikipedia and Wikidata

Importance:

- Improves user experience by providing quick answers
- Helps Google understand context and intent of queries
- Can reduce click-through rates to websites

Becoming an Entity:

- Establish profiles on major social networks
- Implement schema markup on your website
- Create a Google Business Profile
- Add an entry on Wikidata.org

- Aim for a Wikipedia page (if notable)
- Build brand awareness and authority

SEO Implications:

- May decrease organic traffic for some queries
- Emphasizes the importance of structured data
- Encourages focus on entity-based SEO strategies

The Knowledge Graph represents Google's shift towards understanding semantic relationships and providing direct answers. While it can pose challenges for traditional SEO, it also offers opportunities for businesses to enhance their visibility and credibility in search results.

Google Knowledge Panel

An information box displayed on the right side of Google's search results page (SERP) that provides a quick overview of an entity (person, place, organization, or thing).

Key features:

- Powered by Google's Knowledge Graph
- Automatically generated from various web sources
- Displays key information about the search query entity

Content:

- Basic facts (e.g., name, description, type)

- Images
- Social media links
- Related entities

Importance:

- Enhances user experience by providing quick information
- Increases visibility and credibility for featured entities
- Can reduce click-through rates to websites

Getting a Knowledge Panel:

- Cannot be directly created or purchased
- Requires Google to recognize the entity as notable
- Improved chances through:
- Comprehensive website information
- Proper schema markup
- Active social media presence
- Wikipedia/Wikidata entries
- Google Business Profile (for businesses)

Editing:

- Changes can be suggested by verified representatives
- Google reviews and verifies suggested edits

Knowledge Panels represent Google's efforts to provide immediate, authoritative information to users. While beneficial for visibility, they can impact organic traffic to websites by answering queries directly in search results.

Google Penalty

A manual action taken by Google against websites that violate its webmaster quality guidelines. Key points:

- Also known as "manual actions"
- Results in lower rankings or removal from search results
- Distinct from algorithmic changes

Common Causes:

- Unnatural inbound or outbound links
- Thin or auto-generated content
- Hidden text or links
- Cloaking or sneaky redirects

Importance:

- Can significantly reduce website visibility and traffic
- Affects credibility and revenue

Prevention:

- Adhere to Google's webmaster guidelines
- Focus on quality content creation
- Use white-hat SEO techniques
- Regularly audit website for potential issues

Detection and Recovery:

- Check Google Search Console for notifications
- Address issues promptly if penalized
- Submit reconsideration request after fixing problems

Google Penalties are serious consequences for violating search quality guidelines. Understanding and avoiding these penalties is crucial for maintaining a website's search visibility and overall online success. Regular monitoring and adherence to best practices are key to preventing penalties.

Google Sandbox

A theoretical concept in SEO suggesting that new websites may experience difficulty ranking well in Google search results for a period of time after their creation.

Key points:

- Not officially confirmed by Google
- Typically associated with new domains
- May last several months to a year

Possible Explanations:

- Google's caution towards new sites to prevent spam
- Natural time needed for new sites to establish authority

- Lack of backlinks and content for new sites

SEO Implications:

- New sites may experience slow initial growth in search visibility
- Emphasizes the importance of patience in SEO strategies

Best Practices for New Sites:

1. Focus on creating high-quality, relevant content
2. Implement solid on-page SEO techniques
3. Build natural, high-quality backlinks over time
4. Engage in consistent, white-hat SEO practices

While the existence of a Google Sandbox is debated, the concept highlights the challenges new websites face in achieving quick search visibility. It underscores the importance of long-term SEO strategies and the time required to establish credibility and authority in search rankings.

GSC Google Search Console

A free web service by Google that helps website owners monitor and maintain their site's presence in Google Search results.

Key features:

- Performance reports on search visibility and traffic

- Crawl error detection and resolution tools
- Sitemap submission and indexing status checks
- Mobile usability and Core Web Vitals reports
- Manual actions and security issues notifications
- International targeting options
- Backlink analysis

Importance:

- Provides insights into search performance
- Helps identify and fix technical SEO issues
- Facilitates communication with Google about site changes

Best Practices:

1. Choose appropriate property type (URL-prefix or Domain)
2. Regularly monitor Coverage report for indexing issues
3. Address critical errors promptly
4. Use in conjunction with other SEO tools for comprehensive analysis

Originally launched as Google Webmaster Tools in 2006, it was rebranded to Google Search Console in 2015 to reflect its broader user base. It's an essential tool for SEO professionals, webmasters, and site owners to optimize their website's search performance and maintain technical health.

. . .

GOOGLE WEBMASTER GUIDELINES (Google Search Essentials) - https://developers.google.com/search/docs/essentials

A set of best practices and recommendations provided by Google to help website owners and managers optimize their sites for Google's search engine.

KEY COMPONENTS:

TECHNICAL REQUIREMENTS:

- Discoverable and accessible pages
- Live pages (200 HTTP status code)
- Meaningful content

Quality Guidelines:

- Avoid deceptive practices (e.g., cloaking, keyword stuffing)
- Steer clear of link schemes
- Prevent malware and malicious behaviors
- Avoid spammy auto-generated content

Key Best Practices:

1. Create high-quality, user-focused content
2. Ensure proper site structure and navigation
3. Implement accurate metadata

Importance:

- Helps websites align with Google's expectations
- Improves chances of proper crawling, indexing, and ranking
- Reduces risk of penalties or manual actions

Adherence to these guidelines is crucial for maintaining good standing with Google and optimizing a website's search performance. While not exhaustive, following these guidelines forms the foundation of ethical and effective SEO practices.

Googlebot

Google's web crawler that discovers, analyzes, and indexes web pages for Google's search engine.

Key features:

- Main versions: Googlebot Desktop and Googlebot Smartphone
- Smartphone version is primary crawler for mobile-first indexing
- Continuously crawls the web to find new and updated content

Importance:

- Essential for website visibility in Google search results
- Determines which pages are indexed and potentially ranked

Best practices for Googlebot-friendly websites:

1. Optimize robots.txt file
2. Submit and maintain sitemaps
3. Use crawler directives appropriately
4. Implement effective internal linking
5. Regularly audit for crawlability and indexability issues

Identification:

- User agent token: Googlebot
- Full user agent string includes specific details for verification

Understanding Googlebot's function and optimizing for its crawling is crucial for SEO success. Webmasters should ensure their sites are easily discoverable and accessible to Googlebot while using tools like Google Search Console to monitor crawling and indexing status.

Grey Hat SEO

A set of search engine optimization practices that fall between white hat (approved) and black hat (prohibited) techniques.

Key points:

- Combines both Google-approved and violating methods

- Riskier than white hat but less risky than black hat SEO

Common Grey Hat Tactics:

- Buying backlinks
- Moderate keyword stuffing
- Content spinning or auto-generation
- Using private blog networks (PBNs)
- Negative SEO against competitors

Risks:

- Potential for Google penalties
- Short-term gains but long-term risks
- Damage to site credibility and rankings

Alternative White Hat Approaches:

- Guest blogging for quality backlinks
- Creating comprehensive, user-focused content
- Building genuine relationships for link building
- Focusing on search intent and user experience

While grey hat SEO might offer quick wins, it's generally discouraged for long-term SEO strategies. Understanding these tactics is important for identifying and avoiding risky practices, especially when working with SEO contractors or analyzing competitor strategies.

Guest Blogging

The practice of writing and publishing a blog post on someone else's website or blog.

KEY POINTS:

- Author typically receives credit and a backlink in the byline
- Mutually beneficial for both guest blogger and host site

Benefits:

- Builds industry relationships
- Exposes brand to new audiences
- Drives referral traffic
- Establishes thought leadership
- Creates potential SEO-boosting backlinks

Best Practices:

1. Pitch relevant websites with engaged audiences
2. Target sites with substantial organic traffic
3. Pitch multiple sites simultaneously
4. Craft personalized, value-focused pitches

Considerations:

- Most guest blogging is unpaid
- Quality and relevance are crucial for SEO benefits
- Avoid low-quality, spammy guest posting practices

Guest blogging remains a valuable strategy for content marketing, brand building, and SEO when done ethically and with a focus on providing value to the host site's audience. It requires careful targeting and high-quality content to be effective in today's competitive digital landscape.

H1 Tag

An HTML heading element used to mark up the main visible title of a web page.

Key points:

- Syntax: <h1>Page Title</h1>
- Usually the largest and most prominent text on a page
- Important for both SEO and user experience

SEO Importance:

- Helps search engines understand page content
- Often used as a ranking factor
- Supports content structure and hierarchy

Best Practices:

1. Use one H1 per page (ideally)
2. Include target keyword naturally
3. Make it descriptive and relevant to page content
4. Doesn't need to match title tag exactly
5. Ensure all important pages have an H1

Considerations:

- Length is flexible, unlike title tags
- Should be visually distinct from other headings (H2, H3, etc.)
- Can be automatically generated by some CMS platforms

The H1 tag plays a crucial role in both SEO and user experience by clearly defining the main topic of a page. While search engines have become more flexible in interpreting multiple H1s, using a single, well-crafted H1 remains a best practice for most websites.

Header Tags

HTML elements used to structure and organize content on a webpage, ranging from H1 to H6 in descending order of importance. Key points:

- H1: Main page title
- H2-H6: Subheadings and subsections

Importance for SEO:

- Improve content readability and user experience
- Help search engines understand page structure
- Can contribute to featured snippets in search results

Best Practices:

1. Use one H1 per page (ideally)

2. Maintain logical hierarchy (H1 > H2 > H3, etc.)
3. Include relevant keywords naturally, avoid stuffing
4. Keep headers concise (3-5 words ideal)
5. Ensure consistent design and formatting

Considerations:

- Distinct from title tags (which appear in browser tabs and SERPs)
- All six levels (H1-H6) available, but H1-H4 most commonly used
- Can be customized with CSS for visual appeal

Header tags play a crucial role in organizing content for both users and search engines. They provide structure, improve readability, and contribute to SEO efforts when used effectively and in accordance with best practices.

Holistic SEO

A comprehensive approach to search engine optimization that considers all aspects of a website and its online presence, rather than focusing on isolated tactics.

Key components:

1. Content Quality: Creating valuable, relevant content
2. User Experience: Ensuring easy navigation and engagement

3. Technical Optimization: Improving site structure and performance
4. On-Page SEO: Optimizing individual pages for keywords and topics
5. Off-Page SEO: Building authority through backlinks and citations

Importance:

- Aligns with search engine goals for quality results
- Improves overall user experience and engagement
- Helps future-proof against algorithm changes

Implementation Strategies:

- Develop high-quality, user-focused content
- Optimize website structure and performance
- Enhance user interface and navigation
- Build authoritative backlinks and online reputation
- Continuously monitor and improve based on analytics

Holistic SEO aims to create a well-rounded, user-centric online presence that naturally performs well in search rankings. By focusing on overall quality and user satisfaction, this approach can lead to more sustainable and long-term SEO success compared to tactics that target individual ranking factors.

•

Inbound Link

A hyperlink from an external website to your website. Also known as backlinks, incoming links, or inlinks.

Key points:

- Crucial factor in search engine rankings
- Seen as a vote of confidence by search engines
- Passes PageRank from the linking page to the linked page

Importance for SEO:

- Builds website authority and credibility
- Improves search engine visibility
- Drives referral traffic

Best Practices:

1. Aim for links from authoritative websites
2. Prioritize relevant, topically-related sources
3. Avoid over-optimizing anchor texts
4. Focus on white-hat link building techniques

. . .

Considerations:

- Quality over quantity is crucial
- "Nofollow" links don't pass PageRank
- Link relevance and context matter

Metrics:

- Domain Rating (DR) can help assess link value
- Consider overall website credibility, not just metrics

Inbound links remain a cornerstone of SEO strategy. While building high-quality inbound links can be challenging, it's essential for improving search rankings and overall online visibility. Focus on earning links through valuable content and genuine relationships rather than manipulative tactics.

Index Bloat

A condition where a website has an excessive number of low-value or unnecessary pages indexed by search engines.

Key points:

. . .

Causes:

- Dynamic URL generation
- Duplicate content
- Thin content pages
- Improper handling of parameters

Negative impacts:

- Wastes crawl budget
- Dilutes site quality signals
- May harm overall search rankings

Detection:

- Use Google Search Console or SEO tools
- Compare intended vs. actual indexed pages

Prevention and resolution:

1. Implement effective robots.txt and meta tags
2. Improve site structure and internal linking
3. Conduct regular content audits
4. Use canonical tags for duplicate content
5. Optimize dynamic page generation

IMPORTANCE:

- Crucial for maintaining SEO effectiveness
- Ensures search engines focus on valuable content

INDEX BLOAT CAN SIGNIFICANTLY HINDER a website's search performance. Addressing this issue involves a combination of technical SEO practices and content quality management. Regular monitoring and optimization are essential to maintain a lean, effective search index that supports overall SEO goals.

INDEXABILITY

The ability of a web page to be discovered, crawled, processed, and included in a search engine's index. Key points:

- Essential for appearing in search results
- Determined by several technical factors

REQUIREMENTS FOR INDEXABILITY:

1. Crawlability: Page must be accessible to search engine bots
2. No "noindex" tag: Page must not have directives preventing indexing

3. Canonical status: Page should be the preferred version among similar pages

Importance:

- Crucial for organic search visibility
- Affects potential for search traffic

Improving indexability:

1. Submit sitemaps to search engines
2. Use URL Inspection tools for individual pages
3. Implement effective internal linking
4. Ensure proper use of robots.txt and meta tags
5. Use self-referencing canonical tags

Considerations:

- Not all pages should be indexed (e.g., login pages, thank you pages)
- Regular audits can help identify indexing issues

Indexability is fundamental to SEO success. It ensures that search engines can find, understand, and include your content in their search results. Proper management of indexability involves both technical SEO knowledge and strategic content decisions.

Internal Link

A hyperlink that connects one page to another within the same website or domain.

Key points:

- Helps establish website structure and hierarchy
- Facilitates navigation for users and search engine crawlers
- Distributes PageRank (link equity) across the website

Importance:

1. Improves user experience and site navigation
2. Aids search engines in discovering and understanding content
3. Influences search rankings by passing link equity
4. Helps generate sitelinks in search results

Best Practices:

1. Use descriptive, relevant anchor text

2. Balance structural (navigation) and contextual links
3. Avoid excessive linking on a single page
4. Regularly audit for broken or ineffective links
5. Identify and leverage new internal linking opportunities

Considerations:

- Orphan pages (no internal links) may still be indexed but lose link equity benefits
- Strategic internal linking can boost important pages' visibility and rankings

Internal linking is a crucial aspect of on-page SEO and website structure. When implemented effectively, it enhances both user experience and search engine optimization, contributing to better site performance in search results.

Keyword Cannibalization

The situation where multiple pages on a website compete for the same search query, potentially diluting SEO effectiveness.

Key points:

- Occurs when two or more pages target the same keyword
- Not always problematic; depends on search intent and overall traffic impact

Identification:

- Use SEO tools to find multiple URLs ranking for the same keyword
- Analyze search intent and traffic performance of competing pages

When it's an issue:

- Similar pages compete for the same search intent
- Overall organic traffic is negatively impacted

Resolution methods:

1. Merge competing pages:
- Combine content onto the best-performing URL
- Redirect other pages to the merged content
2. Delete and redirect:
- Remove less valuable pages
- Redirect to the stronger page

Considerations:

- Not all instances of multiple pages ranking for the same keyword are problematic
- Evaluate impact on overall organic performance before taking action
- Different search intents can justify multiple ranking pages

Keyword cannibalization requires careful analysis to determine if it's truly hurting SEO performance. Proper resolution can consolidate SEO efforts and improve overall search visibility, but unnecessary "fixes" may harm existing traffic patterns.

Keyword Clustering

A keyword research technique that groups semantically related keywords together to form topical clusters.

Key points:

- Groups similar keywords based on topic and search intent
- Aims to optimize content for multiple related keywords simultaneously

Importance:

1. Aligns with modern search engine algorithms' semantic understanding
2. Improves content relevance and depth
3. Enhances potential to rank for multiple related queries
4. Supports topic authority building

Implementation:

- Use SEO tools to identify related keywords
- Analyze search intent across keyword groups
- Create comprehensive content addressing the entire cluster

Benefits:

- More efficient content creation strategy
- Broader keyword coverage with fewer pages
- Improved topical relevance signals to search engines

Considerations:

- Requires understanding of semantic relationships between keywords
- May involve more complex content planning and creation

. . .

KEYWORD CLUSTERING IS a strategic approach to SEO that reflects the evolving nature of search engine algorithms. By focusing on topical clusters rather than individual keywords, it allows for more comprehensive and effective content optimization, potentially leading to improved search visibility across a range of related queries.

KEYWORD DENSITY

The frequency of a specific keyword or phrase within a piece of content, expressed as a percentage of total words.

KEY POINTS:

- Calculation: (Number of keyword occurrences / Total word count) x 100
- No longer considered a significant ranking factor by modern search engines

IMPORTANCE FOR SEO:

- Minimal direct impact on rankings
- Over-emphasis can lead to keyword stuffing, which is detrimental

BEST PRACTICES:

1. Write naturally, focusing on topic coverage rather than keyword repetition
2. Include keywords in key places (title, H1, URL, meta description) when natural
3. Prioritize comprehensive content over keyword frequency

CONSIDERATIONS:

- No "ideal" keyword density exists
- Excessive density (typically over 2%) may indicate unnatural writing
- Focus on user experience and content quality instead

MODERN APPROACH:

- Emphasize semantic relevance and topic coverage
- Use related terms and synonyms to enhance content depth
- Aim for natural language that addresses user intent

WHILE KEYWORD DENSITY was once a focus of SEO, it's now largely obsolete as a metric. Today's SEO best practices prioritize comprehensive, user-focused content that naturally incorporates relevant keywords and related topics.

Keyword Difficulty (KD)

A metric used in SEO to estimate the challenge of ranking on the first page of search results for a specific keyword.

Key points:

- Typically expressed on a scale of 0-100
- Calculation methods vary among SEO tools
- Based on factors like backlink profiles of top-ranking pages

Importance:

- Helps prioritize keyword targets in SEO strategies
- Assists in identifying low-competition opportunities

Ahrefs' KD Calculation:

- Based on backlink profiles of top 10 ranking pages
- Plotted on a logarithmic scale from 0 to 100

. . .

Considerations beyond KD:

1. Estimated backlink requirements
2. Competitor website authority
3. Search intent analysis
4. Content quality of ranking pages

Best Practices:

- Use KD as an initial filter in keyword research
- Combine with manual SERP analysis for accurate assessment
- Consider your website's authority and resources
- Analyze search intent and content quality of top results

While Keyword Difficulty provides a quick estimate of ranking challenge, it should be used in conjunction with other factors for comprehensive keyword evaluation. Manual SERP analysis remains crucial for accurate assessment of ranking potential.

Keyword Ranking

The position of a website or webpage in search engine results pages (SERPs) for a specific keyword or search query. Key points:

. . .

- Measured numerically (e.g., 1st, 2nd, 3rd position)
- Can vary by search engine, location, and time

Importance:

- Higher rankings correlate with increased organic traffic
- Top 3 positions typically receive the majority of clicks

Tracking Methods:

- Google Search Console (average positions)
- SEO tools like Ahrefs (absolute positions)
- Free keyword rank checkers

Improving Rankings:

1. Optimize for search intent
2. Build quality backlinks
3. Create high-quality, relevant content
4. Improve technical SEO aspects

Best Practices:

- Regularly monitor rankings for important keywords
- Analyze competitor rankings for insights
- Focus on user experience and content quality
- Adapt strategies based on SERP features and changes

Considerations:

- Rankings can fluctuate due to algorithm updates
- Different keywords have varying levels of competition
- Local and personalized search can affect rankings

Keyword rankings are a key performance indicator in SEO, reflecting a website's visibility in search results. While important, they should be considered alongside other metrics like organic traffic and conversions for a comprehensive SEO strategy.

Keyword Stemming

A search engine's ability to recognize and understand variations of a root word in search queries and content.

. . .

Key points:

- Allows search engines to match queries with content containing word variations
- Differs from lemmatization, which considers word context

Importance:

- Improves search relevance and accuracy
- Allows for more natural content writing
- Potentially increases content visibility for related queries

SEO Implications:

- Not a direct ranking factor
- Enables content to rank for word variations without exact matches
- Supports more natural, user-focused content creation

Best Practices:

- Write naturally, focusing on user intent
- Avoid forced or artificial use of word variations
- Include relevant synonyms and related terms organically

Considerations:

- Overuse can be interpreted as keyword stuffing

- Different from manual stemming (adding prefixes/suffixes intentionally)
- Can be bypassed in searches by using quotation marks

Keyword stemming reflects search engines' evolving ability to understand language nuances. While it's not a direct ranking factor, understanding stemming can help content creators write more naturally while still optimizing for search visibility across related terms and phrases.

Keyword Stuffing

The practice of excessively and unnaturally inserting target keywords into web content in an attempt to manipulate search engine rankings.

Key points:

- Considered a spam technique by search engines
- Violates Google's webmaster guidelines
- Can occur in content, anchor texts, and URLs

Historical context:

- Once effective when search algorithms were simpler
- Now obsolete and potentially harmful to SEO

NEGATIVE IMPACTS:

- Can lead to manual penalties from search engines
- Degrades user experience and content quality
- May result in lower search rankings

ALTERNATIVES:

1. Use keywords naturally in prominent places (title, H1, meta description)
2. Focus on high-quality, value-driven content
3. Incorporate relevant secondary keywords and variations
4. Write for users, not search engines

BEST PRACTICES:

- Prioritize content quality over keyword frequency
- Use synonyms and related terms
- Ensure content reads naturally
- Focus on comprehensive topic coverage

KEYWORD STUFFING IS AN OUTDATED and risky SEO tactic. Modern search engine algorithms prioritize content quality and relevance over keyword frequency. SEO professionals should focus on creating valuable, user-focused content that naturally incorporates relevant keywords and topics.

Keywords

Words or phrases that describe the content of a web page, used to optimize content for search engines and target ads.

Key points:

- In SEO: Terms targeted by content creators
- In PPC: Words used for ad targeting
- Different from "search terms" (what users actually type)

Importance:

- Connect user searches to relevant content
- Essential for organic search traffic
- Crucial for effective PPC campaigns

Targeting Keywords:

1. In SEO:

- Include in title, H1, URL, meta description
- Use naturally throughout content
- Optimize images and internal links

. . .

2. In PPC:

- Select relevant keywords for ad campaigns
- Consider quality score for cost-effectiveness

Types:

- Long-tail: Specific phrases with lower search volume
- Short-tail: Broader terms with higher search volume
- Primary: Main topic of the content
- Secondary: Related terms supporting the primary keyword

Best Practices:

- Conduct thorough keyword research
- Focus on relevance and user intent
- Use variations and related terms naturally
- Avoid keyword stuffing

Understanding and effectively using keywords is fundamental to both SEO and PPC strategies. It involves balancing search volume, competition, and relevance to create content and campaigns that meet user needs and business goals.

Landing Page

A standalone web page designed specifically for a marketing or advertising campaign, where visitors arrive after clicking a link from an external source.

Key characteristics:

- Single focused objective
- Clear call-to-action (CTA)
- Minimal navigation options
- Tailored to a specific audience or campaign

Purpose:

- Convert visitors into leads or customers
- Encourage specific actions (e.g., sign-ups, purchases)
- Collect user information

Key Elements:

1. Compelling headline
2. Persuasive copy
3. Relevant imagery

4. Prominent CTA button
5. Form for data collection (if applicable)

Best Practices:

- Ensure message consistency with the referring link
- Optimize for fast loading speed
- Use A/B testing to improve performance
- Make it mobile-friendly
- Include social proof or testimonials

Metrics to Track:

- Conversion rate
- Bounce rate
- Time on page
- Form completion rate

Landing pages are crucial tools in digital marketing, designed to maximize conversion rates by providing a focused, distraction-free environment for visitors to take desired actions. Their effectiveness is key to the success of many online marketing campaigns.

LSA - Latent Semantic Analysis

A natural language processing technique that analyzes relationships between documents and terms to uncover underlying (latent) conceptual meanings. Key points:

- Based on the principle that words in similar contexts have similar meanings
- Uses mathematical techniques to identify patterns and relationships

PROCESS:

1. Create a term-document matrix
2. Apply singular value decomposition (SVD)
3. Reduce dimensions to capture essential relationships

SEO IMPLICATIONS:

- Helps search engines understand content context
- Encourages creation of semantically rich content
- Reduces effectiveness of keyword stuffing

BENEFITS:

- Improves information retrieval accuracy
- Enhances content understanding

- Informs content development strategies

Applications:

- Search engine algorithms
- Content optimization
- Topic modeling
- Semantic search

LSA is crucial in modern SEO as it allows for a more nuanced understanding of content beyond simple keyword matching. It encourages the creation of comprehensive, contextually relevant content that naturally incorporates related terms and concepts, aligning with how search engines interpret and rank web pages.

Link Bait

Content specifically created to attract backlinks from other websites naturally.

Key points:

- Designed to be interesting, useful, or valuable
- Aims to increase website authority and search rankings
- Requires promotion for effectiveness

. . .

Common types:

1. Infographics
2. Original research and studies
3. Comprehensive guides
4. Industry statistics
5. Free tools or resources

Importance for SEO:

- Generates high-quality backlinks
- Improves domain authority
- Increases organic search visibility

Best practices:

- Create unique, high-quality content
- Address audience needs or interests
- Ensure content is easily shareable
- Promote content actively
- Update regularly to maintain relevance

Considerations:

- Quality over quantity in link attraction

- Align with overall content strategy
- Avoid manipulative or deceptive tactics

Link bait is a strategic approach to content creation that aims to naturally attract backlinks, enhancing a website's SEO performance. While effective, it requires a balance of creativity, value provision, and active promotion to succeed in generating quality backlinks and improving search rankings.

Link Building

The process of acquiring hyperlinks from other websites to your own, with the goal of improving search engine rankings and visibility.

Key points:

- Essential component of SEO strategy
- Focuses on acquiring high-quality, relevant backlinks
- One of Google's top ranking factors

Importance:

- Improves search engine rankings
- Increases website authority
- Drives referral traffic

. . .

CHARACTERISTICS OF GOOD LINKS:

1. Dofollow attribute
2. Relevance to your content/niche
3. Appropriate anchor text
4. From authoritative websites

COMMON WHITE-HAT METHODS:

- Creating high-quality, linkable content
- Guest blogging on reputable sites
- Broken link building
- Resource page link building
- Social media promotion

BEST PRACTICES:

- Focus on quality over quantity
- Aim for natural link profiles
- Avoid manipulative or paid link schemes
- Regularly monitor backlink profile

LINK BUILDING IS a crucial aspect of SEO that requires ongoing effort and strategy. While challenging, effective link building can significantly improve a website's search visibility and authority. It's important to focus on ethical, white-hat techniques to ensure long-term success and avoid search engine penalties.

Link Equity (Link Juice)

The authority or value passed from one webpage to another through hyperlinks. Key points:

- Contributes to a page's PageRank and search engine rankings
- Applies to both internal and external links
- Quality and relevance of the link source affect the equity passed

Factors influencing link equity:

1. PageRank of the referring page
2. Relevance of the linking page to the linked page
3. Domain authority of the referring website
4. Overall trustworthiness of the referring site
5. Indexability of the linking page
6. Number of outgoing links on the referring page
7. Relevance of the anchor text

Importance:

- Helps determine a page's authority and potential to rank
- Guides link building strategies

Considerations:

- Cannot be directly measured, only estimated
- Passing link equity doesn't diminish the linking page's value
- Can be controlled using "nofollow" attributes

Understanding link equity is crucial for effective SEO and link building strategies. It emphasizes the importance of acquiring high-quality, relevant backlinks rather than focusing solely on quantity. Properly leveraging link equity can significantly improve a website's search engine visibility and authority.

Link Exchange (Reciprocal Linking)

The practice of two websites agreeing to link to each other's content, often with the goal of improving search engine rankings. Key points:

- Can occur naturally between related websites
- Excessive use considered a link scheme by search engines

Benefits:

- Potential improvement in search visibility
- Increased referral traffic
- Building relationships with other websites

Risks:

- May violate search engine guidelines if overused
- Can lead to algorithmic devaluation of links
- Possible manual penalties for excessive link exchanges

Best Practices:

1. Focus on relevance and value to users
2. Avoid excessive reciprocal linking
3. Ensure links are editorial and contextual
4. Maintain a natural link profile

Considerations:

- About 40% of websites with good search traffic have some reciprocal links
- Quality and relevance of links matter more than quantity
- Should be part of a diverse link-building strategy

While link exchange can be a legitimate SEO tactic when used sparingly and ethically, it should be approached with caution. The focus should be on creating valuable content and building genuine relationships with other websites in your niche, rather than engaging in excessive reciprocal linking purely for SEO purposes.

. . .

Link Farm

A group of websites created to link to each other artificially, with the intention of manipulating search engine rankings.

Key points:

- Considered a black-hat SEO technique
- Violates search engine guidelines
- Similar to Private Blog Networks (PBNs), but links are internal to the farm

Characteristics:

1. Low-quality or auto-generated content
2. Generic website designs
3. Minimal or fake author information
4. Excessive outbound links
5. Unnatural anchor text patterns

Detection methods:

- Evaluate overall website quality
- Check author and "About" information
- Analyze number of linked domains
- Examine anchor text patterns
- Look beyond SEO metrics (e.g., organic traffic history)

Risks:

- Potential for search engine penalties

- Can harm SEO of linked websites
- May lead to manual actions from Google

Best practices:

- Avoid acquiring links from suspected link farms
- Focus on natural, high-quality link building
- Regularly audit backlink profile for low-quality links

Link farms are a manipulative SEO tactic that can lead to severe consequences for websites involved. Understanding how to identify and avoid link farms is crucial for maintaining a healthy backlink profile and adhering to search engine guidelines.

Link Juice

The ranking power or authority passed from one webpage to another through hyperlinks.

Key points:

- Also known as "link equity"
- Contributes to a page's ability to rank in search results
- Quality of the linking page affects the value transferred

Factors influencing link juice:

1. Authority of the linking page/website

2. Relevance of the linking page to the linked content
3. Type and placement of the link
4. Anchor text used in the link

Importance for SEO:

- Helps improve search engine rankings
- Distributes authority across a website
- Signals credibility and relevance to search engines

Best practices to increase link juice:

1. Obtain high-quality backlinks from authoritative sites
2. Implement effective internal linking strategies
3. Use relevant, descriptive anchor texts
4. Create valuable, linkable content

Considerations:

- Not all links pass equal amounts of link juice
- "Nofollow" links typically don't pass link juice
- Excessive outbound links can dilute link juice

Understanding and leveraging link juice is crucial for effective SEO strategies. It emphasizes the importance of quality over quantity in link building and highlights the interconnected nature of web authority in search engine algorithms.

. . .

LINK POPULARITY What is Link Popularity? Link popularity is the measure of the quantity and quality of the backlinks pointing to a website or webpage. It is used in SEO as a relative metric to compare

pasted

A

Here's a concise definition of Link Popularity, styled for a book's glossary:

Link Popularity A measure of the quantity and quality of backlinks pointing to a website or webpage. Key points:

- Indicates the strength of a site's backlink profile
- Used as a relative metric to compare websites' authority
- Influences search engine rankings

Importance:

- Reflects website's perceived authority and trustworthiness
- Contributes to higher search engine rankings
- Key factor in SEO strategies

Measurement:

- Varies by tool or methodology
- Ahrefs uses Domain Rating (DR) for domains and URL Rating (UR) for pages

Improving Link Popularity:

1. Diversify referring domains
2. Focus on topically relevant links

3. Acquire links from authoritative websites
4. Prioritize followed links

Considerations:

- Quality over quantity in link acquisition
- Not the same as Google's PageRank
- Should be part of a comprehensive SEO strategy

Best Practices:

- Earn links through valuable content creation
- Engage in ethical link building techniques
- Regularly monitor and analyze backlink profile

Link popularity is a crucial concept in SEO, reflecting a website's authority and influencing its search engine performance. While important, it should be considered alongside other SEO factors for a well-rounded optimization strategy.

Link Popularity

A measure of the quantity and quality of backlinks pointing to a website or webpage.

Key points:

- Indicates the strength of a site's backlink profile
- Used as a relative metric to compare websites' authority
- Influences search engine rankings

. . .

Importance:

- Reflects website's perceived authority and trustworthiness
- Contributes to higher search engine rankings
- Key factor in SEO strategies

Measurement:

- Varies by tool or methodology
- Ahrefs uses Domain Rating (DR) for domains and URL Rating (UR) for pages

Improving Link Popularity:

1. Diversify referring domains
2. Focus on topically relevant links
3. Acquire links from authoritative websites
4. Prioritize followed links

Considerations:

- Quality over quantity in link acquisition
- Not the same as Google's PageRank
- Should be part of a comprehensive SEO strategy

. . .

Best Practices:

- Earn links through valuable content creation
- Engage in ethical link building techniques
- Regularly monitor and analyze backlink profile

Link popularity is a crucial concept in SEO, reflecting a website's authority and influencing its search engine performance. While important, it should be considered alongside other SEO factors for a well-rounded optimization strategy.

Link Profile

The complete collection of external backlinks pointing to a website or webpage.

Key points:

- Includes both quantity and quality of backlinks
- Crucial factor in search engine rankings
- Reflects a website's perceived authority and trustworthiness

Importance:

- Influences search engine rankings

- Indicates website credibility
- Can impact organic search traffic

Key aspects to analyze:

1. Link velocity (rate of acquiring new backlinks)
2. Anchor text distribution
3. Organic traffic of linking websites
4. Relevance and authority of linking domains

Best practices:

- Focus on quality over quantity
- Aim for diverse, relevant linking domains
- Avoid link schemes or manipulative practices
- Regularly monitor and audit backlink profile

Tools for analysis:

- Ahrefs Webmaster Tools (free for own sites)
- Professional backlink checkers (e.g., Ahrefs Site Explorer)

Considerations:

- Balance metrics (e.g., Domain Rating) with other factors
- Prioritize topical relevance of linking sites
- Be cautious of sudden spikes or drops in backlinks

A healthy link profile is essential for SEO success, reflecting a website's reputation and influencing its search visibility. Regular analysis and ethical link-building practices are crucial for maintaining and improving a website's link profile.

Link Reclamation

The process of identifying and recovering lost backlinks to a website.

Key points:

- Aims to regain link value and maintain link authority
- Involves outreach to webmasters or content owners
- Can improve or stabilize search engine rankings

Common reasons for lost links:

1. Manual link removal

2. Content updates without preserving links
3. Page deletion or redirection
4. Website closure

Process:

1. Identify lost backlinks using SEO tools
2. Analyze reasons for link loss
3. Prioritize valuable lost links
4. Contact webmasters to request link reinstatement

Benefits:

- Preserves existing link equity
- Maintains or improves search rankings
- Strengthens overall backlink profile

Best practices:

- Regularly monitor backlink profile
- Act quickly when valuable links are lost
- Provide clear value proposition when requesting link restoration
- Focus on high-quality, relevant backlinks

Considerations:

- Not all lost links can be recovered
- Some links may not be worth reclaiming
- Requires ongoing effort and relationship management

Link reclamation is an important aspect of SEO maintenance, helping to preserve a website's link authority and search engine performance. It's a proactive approach to link building that focuses on retaining valuable existing backlinks rather than solely acquiring new ones.

Link Rot

The gradual decay of hyperlinks on the internet, where links cease to point to their original target over time.

Key points:

- Natural phenomenon in web ecosystems
- Results in broken or dead links
- Affects both internal and external links

Common causes:

1. Website restructuring without proper redirects
2. Content deletion

3. Website shutdowns
4. Domain expirations

Importance:

- Impacts user experience
- Affects SEO performance
- Reduces content credibility and usefulness

Detection methods:

- Use of broken link checkers (e.g., Ahrefs Broken Link Checker)
- Regular website audits
- Monitoring of backlink profiles

Prevention and mitigation:

1. Implement proper 301 redirects during site changes
2. Regularly audit and update internal links
3. Use permalink structures that are less likely to change
4. Monitor and update external links in content

Best practices:

- Conduct periodic link checks
- Prioritize fixing broken links on high-traffic pages
- Consider using link management tools
- Update or remove content with excessive outdated links

Link rot is an ongoing challenge in maintaining web content quality and SEO performance. Regular monitoring and proactive link management are essential for mitigating its effects and ensuring long-term content accessibility and relevance.

Link Scheme

Manipulative practices aimed at artificially inflating a website's search engine rankings through unnatural link building.

Key points:

- Violates search engine guidelines
- Includes both inbound and outbound link manipulation
- Can lead to search engine penalties

Common types:

1. Buying or selling links
2. Excessive link exchanges
3. Automated link placements
4. Requiring links in Terms of Service
5. Widely distributed footer/template links
6. Followed links in advertisements
7. Over-optimized anchor text in guest posts or comments

Risks:

- Manual penalties from search engines
- Algorithmic devaluation of links
- Wasted resources on ineffective tactics

Detection:

- Unnatural link patterns
- Sudden spikes in backlink acquisition
- Irrelevant or low-quality linking domains

Best practices to avoid:

- Focus on natural, earned links
- Create valuable, linkable content

- Engage in ethical outreach and relationship building
- Use nofollow attributes where appropriate

Importance of avoidance:

- Maintains long-term SEO health
- Preserves website credibility
- Aligns with search engine best practices

Link schemes are considered black-hat SEO tactics and should be avoided. Search engines are continually improving their ability to detect and penalize such practices. Focusing on creating valuable content and earning links naturally is the recommended approach for sustainable SEO success.

Link Spam

The practice of creating artificial backlinks to manipulate search engine rankings, violating search engine guidelines.

Key points:

- Considered a black-hat SEO tactic
- Violates Google's spam policies
- Can result in search engine penalties

. . .

Common forms:

1. Buying or selling links
2. Automated link generation
3. Excessive link exchanges
4. Optimized links in forum comments
5. Widely distributed links in footers/templates
6. Paid links without proper attributes

Google's countermeasures:

- Penguin algorithm update (2012)
- SpamBrain AI system (2018)
- Regular link spam updates

Risks:

- Manual actions (penalties) from Google
- Algorithmic devaluation of links
- Long-term damage to website credibility

Avoidance strategies:

- Focus on creating link-worthy content
- Engage in ethical link-building practices

- Regularly monitor backlink profile
- Use appropriate link attributes (e.g., nofollow, sponsored)

IMPORTANCE:

- Understanding link spam helps maintain search integrity
- Avoiding link spam is crucial for sustainable SEO

WHILE LINK SPAM may seem tempting for quick SEO gains, it poses significant risks to a website's long-term visibility and credibility. Focusing on white-hat SEO techniques and natural link acquisition is the recommended approach for sustainable search engine success.

LINK TEXT (ANCHOR Text)

The visible, clickable text in a hyperlink on a web page. Key points:

- Usually highlighted or underlined
- Provides context for the linked content
- Important for both user experience and SEO

SEO Importance:

- Helps search engines understand linked page content
- Influences relevance assessment for search queries
- Contributes to overall link profile diversity

Best Practices:

1. Be descriptive and concise
2. Avoid generic phrases (e.g., "click here")
3. Include relevant keywords naturally
4. Ensure seamless integration with surrounding content

User Experience Considerations:

- Clearly indicates link destination
- Improves navigation and content discovery
- Enhances overall readability

Cautions:

- Avoid over-optimization with exact-match keywords
- Maintain a natural, varied anchor text profile

- Be wary of spammy or manipulative practices

Link text plays a crucial role in both guiding users and informing search engines about linked content. Effective use of link text balances descriptive accuracy, user-friendliness, and SEO considerations, while avoiding over-optimization that could trigger search engine penalties.

Link Velocity

The rate at which a website or webpage acquires new backlinks over time.

Key points:

- Typically measured in links or referring domains per month
- Concept originates from a 2003 Google patent
- Debated topic in SEO community

Importance in SEO:

- Not officially recognized as a ranking factor by Google
- Quality and relevance of links are more crucial than acquisition rate
- Rapid, unnatural link growth may raise spam flags

. . .

CONSIDERATIONS:

- Natural link growth patterns vary by website and content type
- Sudden spikes can be normal for viral or timely content
- Focus on steady, organic link acquisition rather than rapid growth

MEASUREMENT:

- Use SEO tools like Ahrefs Site Explorer to track link growth over time
- Compare with competitor link acquisition rates for industry benchmarks

BEST PRACTICES:

- Prioritize quality and relevance of backlinks over quantity or speed
- Focus on creating link-worthy content
- Monitor link profile for any unusual patterns or spikes

While link velocity is a topic of discussion in SEO circles, its direct impact on rankings is unconfirmed. The emphasis should be on acquiring high-quality, relevant backlinks through ethical means rather than focusing solely on the speed of link acquisition.

Local Business Schema

A type of structured data markup that provides detailed information about a local business to search engines.

Key points:

- Based on Schema.org vocabulary
- Helps improve visibility in local search results and Google Maps
- Implemented using JSON-LD script in webpage HTML

Key elements:

1. Business name
2. Address
3. Phone number
4. Opening hours
5. Website URL
6. Business type (e.g., BookStore, Restaurant)

Benefits:

- Enhances search engine understanding of business details

- Improves chances of appearing in rich results
- Supports local SEO efforts

Implementation:

- Used within <script> tags in HTML
- Follows specific Schema.org syntax
- Can be validated using Google's Structured Data Testing Tool

Best practices:

- Include all relevant business information
- Keep data accurate and up-to-date
- Use specific business type when possible
- Implement on all location pages for multi-location businesses

Local Business Schema is an important tool for local SEO, helping businesses provide clear, structured information to search engines. This can lead to improved visibility in local search results and a better representation of the business in search features like knowledge panels and map listings.

```
<script type="application/ld+json">
{
"@context": "https://schema.org",
"@type": "BookStore",
"name": "The Owl's Book Nest",
"address": {
"@type": "PostalAddress",
"streetAddress": "123 Feather Lane",
"addressLocality": "Owltown",
```

```
"addressRegion": "Whispering Woods",
"postalCode": "12345",
"addressCountry": "US"
},
"telephone": "+1234567890",
"openingHours": "Mo-Sa 10:00-18:00",
"url": "https://www.owlsbooknestsstore.com"
}
</script>
```

Local Citation

An online mention of a business's name, address, and phone number (NAP) on websites other than the business's own.

Key points:

- Essential for local SEO
- Can be structured (in directories) or unstructured (in content)
- Helps verify business legitimacy to search engines

Types:

1. Structured: Organized listings in directories
2. Unstructured: Mentions in articles, blogs, or reviews

. . .

Importance:

- Considered a local search ranking factor
- Improves business visibility in local searches
- Builds trust and credibility with search engines

Building strategies:

1. Submit to major data aggregators
2. List on popular citation sources (e.g., Yelp, Yellow Pages)
3. Target industry-specific and local directories
4. Seek unstructured citation opportunities

Best practices:

- Maintain consistent NAP information across all citations
- Regularly update and verify citation accuracy
- Focus on quality and relevance over quantity
- Include additional details when possible (e.g., business hours, website)

Local citations play a crucial role in local SEO by helping search engines verify business information and determine local relevance. A strong citation profile can significantly improve a business's visibility in local search results.

Local Pack

A Google Search Engine Results Page (SERP) feature that displays a map and three local business listings for queries with local intent.

Key points:

- Also known as Map Pack, Snack Pack, or Google 3-Pack
- Appears at the top of SERPs for local searches
- Includes business name, address, phone number, and ratings

Importance:

- Increases visibility for local businesses
- Provides quick, relevant information to searchers
- Drives local traffic and potential customers

Ranking factors:

1. Google My Business profile optimization
2. Proximity to searcher
3. Relevance to search query

4. Business prominence (reviews, citations)

Optimization strategies:

1. Create and optimize Google My Business profile
2. Ensure NAP (Name, Address, Phone) consistency across the web
3. Encourage and respond to customer reviews
4. Implement local SEO best practices

Benefits:

- Higher click-through rates compared to standard organic results
- Improved local search visibility
- Enhanced user experience for local searchers

The Local Pack is a crucial element for local businesses seeking to improve their online visibility. It offers a prime position in search results, making it an essential target for local SEO strategies.

Local Search Marketing

The process of optimizing a local business's online presence to improve visibility in local search results.

. . .

Key points:

- Targets customers in a specific geographic area
- Combines SEO, paid search, and online listing management
- Critical for businesses serving customers in person

Importance:

- High conversion potential for local searches
- Increased mobile search relevance
- Drives foot traffic to physical locations

Best practices:

1. Conduct local keyword research
2. Optimize Google Business Profile
3. Manage local citations (NAP consistency)
4. Implement on-page local SEO
5. Utilize paid search for local keywords

Key components:

- Google Business Profile optimization
- Local citation management
- Website optimization for local search

- Local content creation
- Online review management

Tracking:

- Use rank tracking tools for local search positions
- Monitor Google Business Profile insights
- Analyze local search traffic and conversions

Local search marketing is essential for businesses targeting local customers. It combines various digital marketing strategies to improve visibility in local search results, driving both online and offline conversions. Effective local search marketing can significantly impact a business's local presence and customer acquisition.

Local SEO

A specialized branch of search engine optimization focused on improving a business's visibility in local search results.

Key points:

- Targets searches with local intent
- Crucial for businesses serving specific geographic areas

- Incorporates both organic results and map pack listings

Key components:

1. Google Business Profile optimization
2. Local keyword research and on-page optimization
3. Local citation management
4. Customer review acquisition and management

Importance:

- Increases visibility for local searches
- Drives foot traffic to physical locations
- Improves online-to-offline conversions

Best practices:

- Maintain consistent NAP (Name, Address, Phone) information across the web
- Create location-specific website content
- Encourage and respond to customer reviews
- Optimize for "near me" and location-based searches

Tools and features:

- Google Business Profile
- Local citation directories
- Map pack results in SERPs
- Location-based keywords in content

Local SEO is essential for businesses targeting customers in specific geographic areas. It combines traditional SEO techniques with location-specific strategies to improve visibility in both organic search results and map listings, ultimately driving more local customers to a business.

LSI Keywords (Latent Semantic Indexing Keywords)

Words and phrases that are semantically related to a main keyword, helping search engines understand the context and topic of a webpage.

Key points:

- Not synonyms, but contextually related terms
- Based on Latent Semantic Indexing technology
- Not officially recognized by Google as a ranking factor

Importance:

- Helps search engines understand content context
- Improves content relevance and quality
- May indirectly influence search rankings

Finding LSI Keywords:

1. Google's "Related Searches"
2. Google Autocomplete
3. LSI keyword generator tools
4. SEO tools like Ahrefs' Keywords Explorer

Best practices:

- Use naturally in content
- Focus on relevance to the main topic
- Avoid keyword stuffing
- Enhance content comprehensiveness

Considerations:

- Not a direct ranking factor according to Google
- Should complement, not replace, primary keyword strategy
- Helps create more natural, user-friendly content

WHILE THE TERM "LSI KEYWORDS" is widely used in SEO, it's important to note that modern search engines likely use more advanced methods to understand content context. However, incorporating semantically related terms can still improve content quality and potentially aid in search visibility.

METADATA

Data that provides information about other data, often describing attributes of a document, such as an HTML page.

KEY POINTS:

- Includes title tags, meta descriptions, OpenGraph, and TwitterCard data
- Describes content and provides context to services and bots
- Can dictate how a webpage is presented on social media platforms

IMPORTANCE:

- Helps search engines and services understand webpage content
- Enhances visibility in search engines and social media shares
- Structured data (like schema.org) improves content indexing and rich result eligibility

. . .

Best practices:

- Ensure metadata accurately reflects page content
- Use structured data to enhance search engine understanding
- Optimize for social media using OpenGraph and TwitterCard tags
- Regularly audit and update metadata for relevance and accuracy
- Avoid duplicate or misleading metadata

Considerations:

- Structured data is a form of metadata, often misunderstood by SEO practitioners
- Metadata doesn't directly influence rankings but improves content discoverability
- Different platforms may interpret or display metadata differently

Metadata is a foundational aspect of SEO, aiding search engines and platforms in understanding and representing your content. Properly optimized metadata can significantly enhance both search visibility and user engagement.

Meta Description

An HTML attribute that provides a brief summary of a webpage's content.

Key points:

- HTML syntax:
- Appears in search engine results pages (SERPs) and social media shares
- Typically limited to 160 characters (120 for mobile)

Importance:

- Helps search engines understand page content
- Can improve click-through rates from SERPs
- Provides context for users before they visit a page

Best practices:

1. Write unique descriptions for each page
2. Match search intent and page content
3. Include relevant keywords naturally
4. Keep within character limits
5. Avoid keyword stuffing or clickbait

Considerations:

- Google may rewrite or ignore meta descriptions
- Not a direct ranking factor, but influences user behavior
- Should be regularly reviewed and updated

While meta descriptions don't directly impact search rankings, they play a crucial role in SEO by influencing click-through rates and providing context to both users and search engines. Effective meta descriptions can significantly enhance a website's visibility and user engagement in search results.

Meta Keywords

An HTML meta tag that lists keywords relevant to a webpage's content.

Key points:

- HTML syntax:
- Originally intended to help search engines understand page content
- No longer considered a ranking factor by major search engines

Historical context:

- Once used as a signal for search engine rankings

- Became a target for spam and manipulation
- Officially deprecated by Google and Bing

Current status:

- Ignored by Google and most major search engines
- May still be used by some smaller search engines or internal site search systems
- Not recommended for modern SEO practices

Considerations:

- Including meta keywords won't harm SEO, but provides no benefit
- Can potentially reveal SEO strategy to competitors if used
- Time and effort better spent on other SEO tactics

Best practice:

- Focus on creating quality content and optimizing other on-page elements
- If used, keep keywords relevant and avoid stuffing

While meta keywords were once an important part of SEO, they are now largely obsolete for search engine optimization purposes. Modern SEO practices focus on creating high-quality, relevant content and optimizing other more influential on-page elements.

Meta Redirect

A client-side method of automatically redirecting users from one webpage to another using HTML meta tags.

Key points:

- Implemented in the section of HTML
- Can be instant or delayed
- Syntax:

Types:

1. Instant: content="0; url=..."
2. Delayed: content="[seconds]; url=..."

Use cases:

- Temporary page redirection
- Displaying messages before redirecting
- Workaround when server-side redirects aren't possible

. . .

SEO considerations:

- Google interprets instant meta redirects as permanent (301-like)
- Delayed meta redirects treated as temporary (302-like)
- Generally less preferred than server-side redirects

Best practices:

- Use server-side redirects (301/302) when possible
- If used, prefer instant over delayed redirects
- Ensure compatibility across browsers
- Use sparingly and with user experience in mind

While meta redirects can be useful in specific situations, they're generally not recommended as a primary redirection method for SEO purposes. Server-side redirects are typically more reliable and SEO-friendly.

Meta Robots Tag

An HTML tag that provides instructions to search engine crawlers about how to handle a webpage.

. . .

Key points:

- Placed in the section of HTML
- Syntax:
- Controls indexing, crawling, and display in search results

Common directives:

1. noindex: Prevents indexing of the page
2. nofollow: Prevents following links on the page
3. noarchive: Prevents caching of the page
4. nosnippet: Prevents displaying snippets in search results

Importance:

- Allows fine-grained control over search engine behavior
- Helps manage which pages appear in search results
- Protects sensitive or low-value pages from indexing

Considerations:

- Robots.txt must allow crawling for meta robots to be read
- X-Robots-Tag header can be used for non-HTML resources
- Different from robots.txt file in function and implementation

IMPLEMENTATION:

- Can be set manually in HTML
- Often managed through SEO plugins in CMS platforms

THE META ROBOTS Tag is a crucial tool for SEO, allowing webmasters to control how search engines interact with and display their web pages. It provides more precise control than robots.txt and is essential for managing a site's visibility in search results.

META TAGS

HTML elements in a webpage's section that provide metadata about the page to browsers and search engines.

KEY POINTS:

- Not visible to users on the page

- Provide information and instructions to search engines and browsers
- Important for SEO and page rendering

Common Meta Tags:

1. Meta Description: Summarizes page content for SERPs
2. Meta Robots: Controls search engine crawling and indexing
3. Meta Viewport: Sets page rendering on mobile devices
4. Meta Charset: Specifies character encoding

SEO Importance:

- Influences how pages appear in search results
- Affects page indexing and crawling
- Can impact click-through rates from SERPs

Best Practices:

- Use unique, relevant meta descriptions for each page
- Implement appropriate meta robots directives
- Ensure meta tags align with page content and purpose

- Regularly review and update meta tags

CONSIDERATIONS:

- Some meta tags (e.g., meta keywords) are obsolete for SEO
- Not all meta tags are recognized or used by all search engines
- Overuse or misuse can be seen as spammy by search engines

META TAGS PLAY a crucial role in communicating page information to search engines and browsers. While not all meta tags directly affect rankings, they are important for overall SEO strategy and user experience.

MIRROR Site

An exact copy of a website hosted on a different server or location.

KEY POINTS:

- Identical in content and structure to the original site
- Hosted on a different URL or server
- Used to improve accessibility and distribute traffic load

. . .

Purpose:

- Reduce network saturation
- Provide alternative access if primary site is down
- Improve download speeds for large files
- Circumvent censorship or geographical restrictions

Importance:

- Enhances global accessibility
- Balances server load
- Improves download speeds
- Supports content preservation

Creation methods:

- Using tools like HTTrack, cURL, or GNU Wget
- Downloading all website files, including HTML, CSS, and media

Considerations:

- Different from backups (focused on accessibility, not recovery)

- May require canonical tags to avoid SEO issues
- Legal implications if done without permission

Best practices:

- Obtain permission before mirroring others' sites
- Regularly update mirror to match the original
- Implement proper SEO measures to avoid duplicate content issues

Mirror sites play a crucial role in ensuring website availability and performance, particularly for high-traffic or globally accessed websites. However, they must be implemented carefully to avoid legal and SEO complications.

Mobile-First Indexing

Google's approach to primarily use the mobile version of a website for crawling, indexing, and ranking in search results.

Key points:

- Prioritizes mobile content over desktop versions
- Implemented due to increased mobile device usage
- Affects how Google crawls and indexes websites

. . .

Importance:

- Reflects shift towards mobile-centric web browsing
- Encourages mobile-friendly website design
- Impacts search engine rankings and visibility

Best practices:

1. Ensure content parity between mobile and desktop versions
2. Use responsive web design
3. Maintain consistent metadata across versions
4. Optimize for mobile page speed and usability
5. Implement mobile-friendly navigation
6. Include structured data on mobile pages

Implementation:

- Gradual rollout by Google since 2016
- Applied to all new websites from July 2019
- Ongoing process for existing websites

Considerations:

- Desktop-only sites can still be indexed, but may be at a disadvantage
- Regular mobile usability checks are recommended
- Use tools like Google Search Console to monitor mobile performance

Mobile-First Indexing represents a significant shift in how search engines evaluate and rank websites, emphasizing the importance of mobile optimization in modern SEO strategies.

NAP (Name, Address, Phone Number)

The core business information consisting of a company's Name, Address, and Phone number.

Key points:

- Essential for local SEO and online business listings
- Critical for accuracy and consistency across the web

Importance:

1. Impacts local search rankings
2. Builds business credibility

3. Enhances customer trust and accessibility
4. Crucial for Google Business Profile optimization

Best practices:

- Maintain consistent NAP across all platforms
- Regularly audit and update information
- Include NAP in structured data on website
- Ensure accuracy in online directories and citations

Applications:

- Local business directories
- Google Maps listings
- Social media profiles
- Business websites

Considerations:

- Even minor inconsistencies can affect SEO
- Format should be uniform across all listings
- May include additional elements like website URL or business hours

NAP IS fundamental for local SEO success, directly influencing how easily customers can find and contact a business. Consistent and accurate NAP information across the web is crucial for improving local search visibility and maintaining business credibility.

NLU - Natural Language Understanding

A branch of artificial intelligence and natural language processing focused on enabling machines to comprehend and interpret human language in its spoken or written form.

Key points:

- Aims to grasp context, intent, and nuances of language
- Goes beyond simple keyword recognition

Components:

1. Semantic analysis: Understanding word meanings
2. Syntax analysis: Deciphering grammatical structures
3. Contextual understanding: Recognizing situational relevance
4. Pragmatic analysis: Applying real-world knowledge

SEO Implications:

- Influences how search engines interpret queries and content
- Emphasizes content relevance over keyword density
- Encourages creation of user-focused, contextually rich content

Applications:

- Search engines
- Chatbots and virtual assistants
- Content analysis tools
- Sentiment analysis

Importance:

- Enhances machine-human interactions
- Improves accuracy of information retrieval
- Supports more sophisticated SEO strategies

NLU represents a significant advancement in how machines process and understand human language. For SEO, it underscores the importance of creating high-quality, contextually relevant content that addresses user intent, rather than focusing solely on keyword optimization.

. . .

Natural Link

An external hyperlink from one website to another that is voluntarily placed without any solicitation or compensation.

Key points:

- Also known as organic, earned, or editorial links
- Considered the most valuable type of backlink by search engines
- Result of high-quality, valuable content

Characteristics:

- Voluntarily given by the linking site
- Relevant to the linked content
- Not a result of link-building campaigns or outreach

Importance:

- Signals content quality and relevance to search engines
- Contributes to a website's authority and trustworthiness

- Generally more sustainable and less risky than artificially built links

Acquisition strategies:

1. Create high-quality, shareable content
2. Promote content effectively
3. Build genuine relationships in your industry
4. Establish thought leadership in your niche

Considerations:

- Can be difficult to distinguish from well-executed link building
- Takes time and consistent effort to acquire
- Quality of linking sites matters more than quantity

Natural links are the ideal form of backlinks in SEO, representing genuine endorsements of content. While they can be challenging to acquire, they form the foundation of a strong, sustainable link profile that aligns with search engine guidelines and best practices.

Negative SEO

The unethical practice of deliberately attempting to

harm a competitor's search engine rankings through manipulative tactics. Key points:

- Often involves creating spam links to the target site
- Can include fake reviews, content theft, or hacking attempts
- Generally considered ineffective by search engines

Potential impacts:

1. Decreased organic search traffic
2. Damaged online reputation
3. Possible search engine penalties

Prevention strategies:

- Regular backlink profile audits
- Monitoring for lost high-quality backlinks
- Implementing strong website security measures

Best practices:

1. Use SEO tools to track backlink profiles
2. Set up alerts for sudden changes in backlinks

3. Consider disavowing suspicious links
4. Maintain robust website security

CONSIDERATIONS:

- Search engines claim to ignore most negative SEO attempts
- Effectiveness is debated in the SEO community
- May still pose risks to website reputation and security

WHILE NEGATIVE SEO is generally considered ineffective due to search engine algorithms' ability to detect and ignore spam, website owners should remain vigilant and implement protective measures to safeguard their online presence and reputation.

NOFOLLOW

An HTML link attribute that instructs search engines not to pass link equity or PageRank to the linked page.

KEY POINTS:

- Syntax: rel="nofollow"
- Introduced by Google in 2005 to combat comment spam

- Does not influence search rankings of linked pages

USAGE:

- User-generated content (comments, forums)
- Paid or sponsored links
- Links to untrusted content

HTML EXAMPLE:

<a href="https://andrewbus.com" rel="nofollow">Andrew Bus</a>

SEO IMPLICATIONS:

- Helps manage link equity flow
- Protects against potential penalties for paid links
- May be used in black-hat SEO to create "natural" link profiles

RELATED ATTRIBUTES:

- rel="sponsored" for paid links
- rel="ugc" for user-generated content

Best practices:

- Use on paid or untrusted external links
- Avoid on internal links to important pages
- Regularly audit nofollow links on your site

Considerations:

- Google may treat nofollow as a "hint" rather than a directive
- Nofollow links can still drive referral traffic
- Overuse may impact natural link profile appearance

Understanding and properly implementing nofollow attributes is important for maintaining a healthy link profile and adhering to search engine guidelines, particularly for managing external links and paid partnerships.

Noindex Tag

An HTML meta tag or HTTP header directive that instructs search engines not to include a specific web page in their search results.

Key points:

- Prevents indexing of specific pages

- Can be implemented via meta tag or X-Robots-Tag

SYNTAX:

Meta tag:
X-Robots-Tag: X-Robots-Tag: noindex

USAGE:

- Private or login-required pages
- Thank you pages
- Low-quality or thin content pages
- Duplicate content (though canonicalization is preferred)

BEST PRACTICES:

1. Ensure page is crawlable (not blocked by robots.txt)
2. Use cautiously, as it affects link equity flow
3. Regularly audit noindexed pages
4. Prefer canonical tags for duplicate content

SEO IMPLICATIONS:

- Removes pages from search results

- Long-term use may lead to loss of link equity
- Can help focus crawl budget on important pages

Considerations:

- Takes time to be effective after implementation
- May still allow page to be crawled initially
- Should be used strategically to avoid accidental removal of important pages

The noindex tag is a powerful tool for controlling which pages appear in search results. When used correctly, it can improve a site's SEO by focusing search engines on the most valuable content.

Noopener

An HTML link attribute that enhances security when linking to external websites, especially those opening in new tabs or windows.

Key points:

- Syntax: rel="noopener"
- Prevents linked pages from accessing the original page through JavaScript
- Protects against potential phishing or malicious redirects

. . .

HTML EXAMPLE:

<a href="https://andrewbus.com" rel="noopener" target="_blank">Best SEO tool</a>

IMPORTANCE:

- Enhances user security
- Prevents potential exploitation of window.opener property
- Recommended for all external links opening in new tabs/windows

SEO IMPACT:

- No direct effect on search engine optimization
- Does not affect link equity or crawling

IMPLEMENTATION:

- Automatically added in WordPress since 2017
- Modern browsers apply noopener behavior to target="_blank" links
- Can be manually added to links for older browser compatibility

Best practices:

- Use on all external links opening in new tabs/windows
- Combine with careful selection of linked websites
- Consider using alongside rel="noreferrer" for additional privacy

While noopener doesn't directly impact SEO, it's an important security feature that enhances user protection when navigating away from your site. Its use is recommended as part of overall web security best practices.

Noreferrer

An HTML link attribute that prevents the browser from sending referrer information to the linked website when a user clicks the link.

Key points:

- Syntax: rel="noreferrer"
- Blocks referrer data from being sent to the target website
- Also implies noopener functionality for security

HTML example:

```
<a href="https://example.com" rel="noreferrer" target="_blank">Link text</a>
```

Functionality:

- Hides the origin of the traffic from the linked site
- Visits appear as direct traffic in analytics tools
- Provides an additional layer of privacy for users

SEO implications:

- No direct impact on search engine rankings
- Does not affect link equity or crawlability
- May impact referral traffic tracking for linked sites

Use cases:

- Enhancing user privacy
- Preventing referral information leakage
- Additional security measure for external links

Considerations:

- Modern browsers limit referrer information to domain name only
- Can be combined with noopener for maximum security
- May affect analytics accuracy for linked websites

While noreferrer doesn't directly influence SEO, it's a useful tool for enhancing user privacy and security. Its implementation should be considered as part of a broader strategy for managing external links and user data protection.

. . .

Off-page SEO

Search engine optimization activities performed outside of a website to improve its search engine rankings.

Key points:

- Focuses on external factors influencing rankings
- Often synonymous with link building, but encompasses more

Key components:

1. Backlink acquisition
2. Brand mentions and citations
3. Social media presence
4. Online reviews and ratings
5. Guest posting and content marketing

Importance:

- Builds domain authority and credibility
- Improves search engine visibility
- Drives referral traffic

Best practices:

1. Acquire high-quality, relevant backlinks
2. Optimize Google Business Profile for local SEO
3. Encourage and manage online reviews
4. Engage in industry-relevant guest posting
5. Cultivate brand mentions across the web

Considerations:

- Less direct control compared to on-page SEO
- Requires ongoing effort and relationship building
- Quality over quantity in link building and mentions

Off-page SEO complements on-page efforts by building a site's authority and relevance from external sources. While more challenging to control directly, effective off-page SEO strategies can significantly impact a website's overall search performance and visibility.

On-page SEO

The practice of optimizing individual web pages to improve search engine rankings and attract organic traffic.

Key elements:

- Content optimization

- HTML source code optimization
- User experience enhancement

Key components:

1. Title tags and meta descriptions
2. Header tags (H1, H2, etc.)
3. URL structure
4. Image optimization (alt text, file names)
5. Internal and external linking
6. Content quality and relevance

Best practices:

1. Match search intent
2. Use descriptive, keyword-rich titles
3. Create short, meaningful URLs
4. Write compelling meta descriptions
5. Optimize images for search
6. Implement strategic internal linking

Importance:

- Helps search engines understand page content
- Improves user experience and engagement
- Increases chances of ranking for target keywords

. . .

Considerations:

- Requires ongoing maintenance and updates
- Should align with overall SEO strategy
- Balance between optimization and natural content flow

On-page SEO is a fundamental aspect of search engine optimization, providing direct control over factors that influence a page's visibility and ranking in search results. It forms the foundation for effective off-page SEO efforts and overall search performance.

Open Graph Meta Tags

HTML elements that control how a webpage appears when shared on social media platforms.

Key points:

- Developed by Facebook in 2010
- Used by various social networks (e.g., Facebook, Twitter, LinkedIn)
- Enhances the appearance of shared links

Essential tags:

1. og:title - Page title
2. og:type - Content type (e.g., article, video)
3. og:url - Canonical URL
4. og:image - Featured image URL
5. og:description - Brief content description

IMPORTANCE:

- Controls shared content presentation
- Improves click-through rates from social media
- Ensures correct information display

IMPLEMENTATION:

- Added to the section of HTML
- Can be managed through CMS plugins (e.g., Yoast SEO for WordPress)
- Customizable for different social platforms

BEST PRACTICES:

- Use high-quality, appropriately sized images
- Write compelling titles and descriptions
- Ensure consistency with on-page content
- Regularly test using platform-specific debugging tools

. . .

Open Graph Meta Tags are crucial for optimizing how content appears when shared on social media. They provide webmasters control over the visual representation of their pages, potentially improving engagement and traffic from social platforms.

Organic Search Results

The unpaid listings that appear on a search engine results page (SERP) in response to a user's query.

Key points:

- Determined by search engine algorithms
- Exclude paid advertisements
- Include various SERP features (e.g., featured snippets, local results)

Importance:

- Provide relevant, trustworthy information to users
- Cost-effective traffic source for websites
- Crucial for search engine user experience and revenue

Key characteristics:

- Based on relevance and quality of web pages
- Not influenced by advertising payments
- Can include rich snippets and enhanced listings

Ranking factors:

1. Website crawlability and indexability
2. Content quality and relevance
3. On-page SEO optimization
4. Backlink profile
5. User experience signals

Best practices for ranking:

- Create high-quality, SEO-optimized content
- Implement thorough on-page SEO
- Build a strong, relevant backlink profile
- Ensure website technical health
- Focus on user experience and engagement

Organic search results are the cornerstone of search engine optimization (SEO). They represent the primary way websites can attract targeted, high-quality traffic without direct advertising costs. Understanding and optimizing for organic search is crucial for long-term online visibility and success.

Orphan Page

A webpage on a website that has no internal links pointing to it from other pages on the same site.

Key points:

- Accessible only via direct URL or external links
- Can be intentional or accidental
- Often overlooked in site structure

Types:

1. Deliberate: e.g., special landing pages, hidden content
2. Accidental: result of site migrations, redesigns, or errors

SEO implications:

- Reduced discoverability by search engines
- Lower PageRank due to lack of internal link equity
- Potential indexing issues

. . .

Causes:

- Site migrations or redesigns
- CMS errors
- Outdated content
- Testing pages

Detection methods:

- SEO crawling tools (e.g., Ahrefs Site Audit)
- Comparing sitemap/analytics data with crawl data

Resolution:

- Add internal links to valuable orphan pages
- Remove or noindex irrelevant orphan pages
- Redirect obsolete orphan pages

Best practices:

- Regularly audit site structure
- Implement proper internal linking strategy
- Ensure important pages are linked from site navigation

. . .

WHILE SOME ORPHAN pages are intentional, accidental ones can harm SEO efforts. Regular site audits and proper internal linking strategies are crucial for maintaining a healthy site structure and maximizing SEO potential.

OUTBOUND LINK

A hyperlink on a webpage that directs users to a different website or domain.

KEY POINTS:

- Also known as external links
- Connects one website to another
- Reciprocal to inbound links (backlinks) for the linked site

PURPOSES:

1. Providing additional resources
2. Citing sources
3. Referencing products (e.g., affiliate marketing)

SEO IMPLICATIONS:

- Passes "link equity" to linked pages

- Can signal topic relevance to search engines
- May influence the linking site's perceived authority

Best practices:

- Use relevant, high-quality outbound links
- Consider using "nofollow" for sponsored or untrusted links
- Maintain a balance between internal and external links

Considerations:

- Excessive outbound linking may dilute page authority
- Links to low-quality sites can negatively impact SEO
- Opening links in new tabs can improve user experience

Outbound links play a crucial role in creating an interconnected web and can contribute to a site's SEO strategy. When used judiciously, they enhance content credibility, provide value to users, and help establish topical relevance for search engines.

. . .

Page Speed

The measure of how quickly a web page loads and becomes fully interactive for users.

Key points:

- Typically measured in seconds
- Critical factor in user experience and SEO
- Influences bounce rates and conversions

Importance:

- Google ranking factor for mobile search since 2018
- Part of Core Web Vitals in Google's page experience signals
- Directly impacts user satisfaction and engagement

Key influencing factors:

1. Web hosting quality
2. Image optimization
3. Caching implementation
4. Code minification
5. Content Delivery Network (CDN) usage
6. Mobile optimization

. . .

Best practices:

- Optimize images and multimedia content
- Leverage browser and server-side caching
- Minify CSS, JavaScript, and HTML
- Use a reliable CDN
- Implement responsive design for mobile

Measurement tools:

- Google PageSpeed Insights
- GTmetrix
- Lighthouse
- WebPageTest

Page speed is a crucial aspect of web performance that affects both user experience and search engine rankings. Optimizing page speed involves a combination of technical improvements and content optimization strategies to ensure fast, efficient loading across all devices.

PageRank (PR)

An algorithm developed by Google co-founders to determine the relative importance and authority of a webpage based on its incoming links.

. . .

Key points:

- Named after co-founder Larry Page
- Part of Google's ranking algorithm since 1997
- No longer publicly visible (removed from Google Toolbar in 2016)

Importance:

- Helps determine page authority and relevance
- Influences search engine rankings
- Basis for modern link-based SEO strategies

Calculation factors:

- Quantity of incoming links
- Quality and authority of linking pages
- Relevance of linking content

Modern equivalents:

- URL Rating (UR) and Domain Rating (DR) in Ahrefs
- Similar metrics in other SEO tools

Best practices:

1. Focus on earning high-quality, relevant backlinks
2. Optimize internal linking structure
3. Fix broken links to preserve link equity
4. Prioritize content quality over link quantity

Considerations:

- Original public metric led to link spam
- Current implementation likely more sophisticated
- Part of a broader set of ranking factors

While no longer publicly visible, PageRank remains a fundamental concept in SEO, emphasizing the importance of quality backlinks and overall link profile strength in determining a page's authority and potential to rank well in search results.

Paid Link

A hyperlink to a website that has been purchased or obtained through monetary compensation.

Key points:

- Often used in attempts to manipulate search engine rankings
- Violates search engine guidelines when used for SEO purposes
- Can take various forms (e.g., sponsored content, advertising, PBNs)

Types:

1. Advertising links
2. Sponsored article links
3. Paid product placements
4. Direct link placements
5. Private Blog Network (PBN) links

SEO implications:

- Violates Google's Webmaster Guidelines
- Can lead to penalties or manual actions
- May result in devaluation of links

Acceptable practices:

- Using "nofollow" or "sponsored" attributes on paid links
- Clearly labeling sponsored content

- Focusing on legitimate advertising rather than SEO manipulation

Risks:

- Search engine penalties
- Loss of search visibility
- Damage to site's authority and credibility

Best practices:

- Avoid buying links for SEO purposes
- Focus on earning natural, high-quality backlinks
- Use appropriate attributes for sponsored content
- Prioritize content quality and user value

While paid links can be legitimate for advertising purposes, their use for manipulating search rankings is against search engine guidelines. SEO professionals should focus on earning natural, high-quality backlinks through valuable content and genuine relationship-building.

Pillar Page

A comprehensive webpage that covers a broad topic in-depth and links to related, more specific content pieces within a content cluster.

. . .

Key points:

- Targets a main keyword for a broad topic
- Acts as a hub for related subtopic pages
- Provides an overview of the entire subject area

Importance:

1. Enhances topical authority
2. Improves internal linking structure
3. Aids in content organization
4. Enhances user navigation and experience

Characteristics:

- In-depth, comprehensive content
- Links to related subtopic pages
- Often longer than standard blog posts
- May include visual elements for better engagement

SEO benefits:

- Strengthens topical relevance signals
- Improves crawling and indexing efficiency

- Potentially attracts more backlinks due to comprehensiveness

Best practices:

- Focus on user value and comprehensive coverage
- Design for visual appeal and easy navigation
- Regularly update with new, relevant information
- Integrate seamlessly with overall content strategy

Pillar pages are a key element in topic cluster strategies, helping to establish topical authority, improve site structure, and enhance user experience. They serve as cornerstone content pieces that can significantly boost a website's SEO performance for broad topic areas.

Pogo-Sticking

A user behavior where searchers rapidly bounce back and forth between search engine results pages (SERPs) and individual search results.

Key points:

- Indicates user dissatisfaction with search results
- Not confirmed as a direct ranking factor by Google
- Can signal content or user experience issues

. . .

Causes:

1. Mismatched search intent
2. Poor web design
3. Subpar user experience
4. Misleading titles or descriptions

SEO implications:

- May indirectly affect rankings through other metrics
- Indicates potential need for content improvement
- Can lead to decreased organic traffic

Prevention strategies:

1. Align content with search intent
2. Improve website design and usability
3. Enhance page load speed
4. Ensure mobile-friendliness
5. Create accurate, non-clickbait titles and meta descriptions

Best practices:

- Regularly analyze user behavior metrics
- Conduct user testing to identify pain points
- Continuously improve content quality and relevance
- Optimize for Core Web Vitals

While not officially a ranking factor, pogo-sticking can indicate issues with content relevance or user experience. Addressing the root causes can lead to improved user engagement, potentially benefiting SEO performance indirectly.

Primary Keyword

The main term or phrase that a webpage is primarily optimized to rank for in search engine results.

Key points:

- Also known as focus keyword or main keyword
- Typically has higher search volume than secondary keywords
- Represents the core topic of the content

Importance:

- Guides content focus and structure
- Signals page topic to search engines

- Often has highest traffic potential among targeted keywords

Selection criteria:

- Relevance to content and audience
- Search volume and competition
- Alignment with overall SEO strategy

Implementation:

1. Include in title tag, H1, and URL
2. Use naturally in content introduction
3. Incorporate in meta description
4. Support with related secondary keywords

Best practices:

- Target one primary keyword per page
- Conduct thorough keyword research
- Balance with secondary keywords for comprehensive coverage
- Prioritize user intent and content quality

Considerations:

- Avoid keyword stuffing
- Ensure natural language use
- Consider long-tail variations for supporting content

PRIMARY KEYWORDS FORM the foundation of on-page SEO strategies, guiding content creation and optimization efforts. While crucial, they should be used in conjunction with secondary keywords to create comprehensive, user-focused content that satisfies search intent.

PRIVATE BLOG NETWORK (PBN)

A group of websites created solely to build backlinks to a main website, with the aim of manipulating search engine rankings.

KEY POINTS:

- Considered a black-hat SEO tactic
- Violates Google's Webmaster Guidelines
- Attempts to artificially boost a site's authority

CHARACTERISTICS:

- Multiple websites under common control
- Low-quality or thin content
- Primarily exists to provide backlinks

. . .

RISKS:

1. Google penalties
2. Devaluation of links
3. Potential de-indexing of main site

REASONS FOR USE:

- Difficulty of natural link building
- Control over anchor text
- Perceived short-term ranking benefits

DETECTION METHODS:

- Analyzing backlink profiles
- Checking for shared hosting or IP addresses
- Identifying unnatural link patterns

BEST PRACTICES:

- Avoid using or purchasing PBN links
- Disavow suspected PBN links cautiously
- Focus on white-hat link building strategies

PBNs ARE a high-risk SEO tactic that can lead to severe penalties from search engines. While they may provide short-term ranking boosts, the long-term risks far outweigh potential benefits. SEO professionals should focus on ethical, sustainable link-building strategies instead.

RankBrain

A machine learning algorithm used by Google to interpret search queries and provide more relevant search results.

Key points:

- Part of Google's core algorithm since 2015
- Uses artificial intelligence to understand context and intent
- Especially effective for new and long-tail queries

Functionality:

- Interprets natural language patterns
- Learns word associations and relationships
- Improves understanding of ambiguous or novel queries

Importance for SEO:

- Enhances Google's ability to match content with user intent
- Reduces reliance on exact-match keywords
- Encourages more natural, conversational content

Best practices:

1. Write content in natural, conversational language
2. Focus on comprehensive topic coverage
3. Prioritize user intent over keyword density
4. Create content that answers related questions

Considerations:

- No specific optimization techniques required
- Emphasis on high-quality, relevant content
- Supports the trend towards semantic search

RankBrain represents a significant shift in how search engines interpret queries and match them with relevant content. It underscores the importance of creating user-focused, natural language content that addresses the intent behind searches rather than focusing solely on specific keywords.

Reciprocal Link

Occurs when two websites link to each other. While reciprocal links can occur naturally, deliberately building them for SEO purposes is discouraged.

Key points:

- Involves mutual linking between two websites
- Natural reciprocal links are harmless, but deliberate ones can violate Google's guidelines
- Excessive link exchanges are considered a black hat SEO practice
- Common across many websites, especially within related niches

Importance:

- Helps foster natural relationships between related websites
- Can contribute to link spam if overused or manipulated
- Google's Spam Policies discourage excessive "link to me and I'll link to you" practices

Best practices:

- Allow reciprocal links to occur naturally, without explicit agreements

- Focus on adding value to users with relevant and useful links
- Avoid mass link exchanges through outreach or agreements
- Audit reciprocal links to ensure they're not part of a deliberate SEO manipulation strategy

CONSIDERATIONS:

- Reciprocal links are common, with studies showing over 73.6% of domains having some form of reciprocal link
- Even if common, deliberate and large-scale reciprocal link schemes can lead to penalties
- Healthy reciprocal links should prioritize content relevance and user value, not rankings

RECIPROCAL LINKS ARE a natural part of the web, especially within related niches. However, SEO practitioners should avoid building reciprocal links with the sole intention of influencing rankings, as this can result in penalties from search engines.

RELATIVE URL

A Uniform Resource Locator (URL) that defines the location of a target relative to the current page, without including the protocol or domain name.

. . .

Key points:

- Refers to the location of a resource based on the address of the current page
- Lacks the protocol (e.g., "http://") and domain name
- Can lead to different destinations depending on whether the URL ends with a trailing slash (directory vs. file)
- Various formats include "./" for the current directory and "../" for one level up

Importance:

- Reduces the need to hard-code the full URL on internal links, making site maintenance easier
- Understanding directory structure is crucial to avoid linking errors
- Commonly used within the same website for internal navigation

Best practices:

- Use relative URLs within your website's content, but absolute URLs for canonical and hreflang tags
- Ensure URLs are accurate by considering whether the page ends with a trailing slash

- Regularly audit links to ensure relative URLs lead to the correct destinations
- Be mindful when moving directories to avoid breaking relative URL links

HTML Syntax Example:

Relative URL with a trailing slash:
<a href="best-practices">best practices</a>
Root-relative URL:
<a href="/best-practices">best practices</a>

Considerations:

- Relative URLs can lead to different pages depending on the directory structure
- No SEO difference between relative and absolute URLs in links
- Using absolute URLs is recommended for rel="canonical" and hreflang tags to avoid confusion

Relative URLs provide flexibility for internal linking but require careful attention to directory structure and placement. While they have no direct SEO impact, proper use helps prevent errors and ensures smooth navigation within a website.

. . .

Resource Pages

Curated collections of links to external resources, such as articles, guides, or tools, designed to provide value to visitors by compiling relevant information in one place.

Key points:

- Contain links to helpful external content or tools
- Popular due to ease of creation and the value they offer to users
- Often used for link-building strategies

Importance:

- Help generate social shares and backlinks for the publisher
- External resource pages are valuable for SEO link-building efforts
- Provide an opportunity to position your content as a helpful resource for other sites

Best practices for resource page link building:

1.Finding Relevant Resource Pages:

- Use Google search operators (e.g., "intitle:resources inurl:links.html")

- Use tools like Ahrefs to extract and analyze search results or reverse-engineer competitor links

2.Vetting Resource Pages:

- Analyze pages for domain rating (DR) and organic search traffic
- Ensure pages are regularly updated and maintained
- Identify gaps where your link would provide the most value

3.Reaching Out:

- Contact the person responsible for the page with relevant, valuable content
- Suggest your link as a replacement for broken links where applicable
- Focus on building genuine relationships by offering useful resources

CONSIDERATIONS:

- Quality and relevance are key when suggesting your content to resource pages
- Resource pages should be actively maintained, otherwise they lose value
- Look for opportunities to fill gaps or replace broken links with your content

. . .

RESOURCE PAGES OFFER both SEO benefits and value to users by providing organized, relevant information. They are also a popular tool for link building when approached strategically.

RICH SNIPPET

A visually enhanced search result that displays additional information from a webpage's structured data, making it more appealing and informative in Google's search results.

KEY POINTS:

- Displays expanded information like ratings, cooking times, or event details
- Generated from structured data types such as reviews, recipes, or events
- Google often uses "rich snippet" and "rich results" interchangeably, though rich snippets are a subset of rich results

IMPORTANCE:

- Increases click-through rates by making results more visually appealing
- Helps users find relevant information faster, improving user experience

- Can make your webpage stand out from competitors in search engine results
- Improves chances of being featured in voice searches with speakable structured data

Best practices for rich snippets:

- Implement structured data relevant to your page content (e.g., reviews, recipes, events)
- Ensure that structured data is accurate and follows Google's guidelines
- Regularly test your structured data with Google's Rich Results Test tool
- Optimize for common user queries to increase the likelihood of appearing as a rich snippet

HTML Syntax Example:

For a review snippet:

```
<SCRIPT TYPE="APPLICATION/LD+JSON">
{
"@context": "https://schema.org",
"@type": "Review",
"itemReviewed": {
"@type": "Product",
"name": "Vegan Kale Salad"
},
"author": {
```

```
"@type": "Person",
"name": "Jane Doe"
},
"reviewRating": {
"@type": "Rating",
"ratingValue": "5",
"bestRating": "5"
}
}
</script>
```

CONSIDERATIONS:

- Structured data helps Google understand your content better, increasing the likelihood of being featured as a rich snippet
- Not every page is eligible for a rich snippet; it depends on the relevance and quality of the structured data
- Optimize for mobile and voice search by including speakable structured data

RICH SNIPPETS PLAY a significant role in improving visibility on SERPs by providing users with more detailed and useful information, enhancing both SEO performance and user engagement.

ROBOTS.TXT

A file that instructs web crawlers on which URLs to

crawl or avoid on a website. It also includes options to control crawling speed for certain crawlers.

Key points:

- Controls web crawler access to specific areas of a website
- Does not control indexing, but limits crawling behavior
- Adhered to by "good" web crawlers; ignored by malicious or unregistered crawlers
- Syntax includes user-agent, disallow, allow, sitemap, and crawl-delay directives

Importance:

- Helps optimize crawl budgets by reducing unnecessary crawling of non-public pages
- Prevents crawling of sections like login pages, PDFs, or gated content
- Can block resource-heavy areas of a site from being crawled
- Not a reliable method for controlling indexing—use meta tags or HTTP headers for that

Best practices for robots.txt:

- Use to block access to non-public or resource-heavy content
- Always combine with other methods (like "noindex" meta tags) for controlling indexing
- Regularly test your robots.txt file using Google Search Console's robots.txt Tester
- Do not block pages you want Google to update, especially if they have "noindex" tags

EXAMPLE OF ROBOTS.TXT SYNTAX:

```
User-agent: AhrefsSiteAudit
Disallow: /resources/
Allow: /resources/images/
Crawl-delay: 2
```

SITEMAP: https://ahrefs.com/academy/sitemap.xml

HOW TO BLOCK AI crawlers bots:

```
user-agent: {AI-Ccrawlers-Bot-Name-Here}
disallow: /
```

HOW TO BLOCK OPENAI BOT:

```
User-agent: GPTBot
Disallow: /
User-agent: ChatGPT-User
Disallow: /
```

. . .

Considerations:

- A blocked URL can still be indexed if Google discovers it through external links
- Ensure you're not blocking important content or resources needed for rendering pages
- Robots.txt is not necessary for all websites, but can be helpful for larger sites or those with complex content structures
- CMS platforms like WordPress automatically generate a basic robots.txt file to block sensitive areas like /wp-admin/

Robots.txt is an essential tool for controlling how search engine crawlers interact with your site. However, it should not be the sole method for managing indexing or controlling which pages appear in search results.

Here's a concise definition of Schema Markup, styled for a book's glossary:

Schema Markup

A standardized format for structured data that helps search engines understand and interpret website content.

Key points:

- Based on vocabulary from Schema.org

- Implemented using JSON-LD, Microdata, or RDFa
- Enhances search engine result presentations

Importance:

- Improves search engine understanding of content
- Enables rich snippets and enhanced search results
- Can increase click-through rates from SERPs

Common types:

1. Article
2. Product
3. FAQ
4. Recipe
5. Event
6. Video

SEO benefits:

- Potential for featured snippets and rich results
- Improved visibility in search results
- Better content interpretation by search engines

. . .

IMPLEMENTATION METHODS:

- WordPress plugins (e.g., Yoast SEO, Rank Math)
- Manual coding in HTML
- Google's Structured Data Markup Helper

BEST PRACTICES:

- Use relevant schema types for your content
- Implement JSON-LD when possible
- Test markup using Google's Rich Results Test
- Keep schema up-to-date with content changes

SCHEMA MARKUP IS a powerful tool for enhancing how search engines interpret and display website content. By providing clear, structured information about page elements, it can significantly improve a site's visibility and performance in search results.

SEARCH ENGINE POISONING

A malicious tactic where attackers manipulate search engine algorithms to rank harmful websites or content in search results.

KEY POINTS:

- Aims to lure users to malicious pages through organic search results
- Uses black-hat SEO techniques to achieve high rankings
- Often targets long-tail or trending keywords

Common techniques:

1. Cloaking
2. Doorway pages
3. Keyword stuffing
4. Link spam
5. Sneaky redirects

Risks to users:

- Malware distribution
- Phishing attempts
- Personal data theft

Protection measures:

1. Use updated antivirus software
2. Keep browsers up-to-date
3. Be cautious of prompts to install software
4. Verify website legitimacy before entering sensitive information

. . .

Search engine response:

- Continuous algorithm updates to detect and penalize manipulative tactics
- Manual review processes for suspicious content
- Collaboration with security firms to identify threats

Importance:

- Highlights the need for user vigilance in online searches
- Underscores the ongoing battle between search engines and malicious actors
- Emphasizes the importance of ethical SEO practices

Search Engine Poisoning represents a significant threat in the digital landscape, exploiting user trust in search results. It underscores the need for both user awareness and ongoing efforts by search engines to maintain the integrity of search results.

Search Engine Results Pages (SERPs)

The web pages displayed by a search engine in response to a user's query.

. . .

Key components:

- Organic results: Algorithmically selected listings
- Paid results: Advertisements
- SERP features: Rich snippets, knowledge panels, etc.

Importance:

- Primary source of organic search traffic
- Reflects search engine's understanding of user intent
- Determines website visibility and click-through rates

Key elements:

1. Title tags
2. Meta descriptions
3. URL structure
4. Rich snippets (when applicable)
5. SERP features (e.g., featured snippets, image packs)

Ranking factors:

- Relevance to search query
- Website authority and quality
- User experience signals
- Content quality and depth

SEO strategies for SERP visibility:

1. Create high-quality, relevant content
2. Optimize on-page elements
3. Build quality backlinks
4. Improve technical SEO aspects
5. Target featured snippets and rich results

SERPs are the battleground of SEO, where websites compete for visibility and user attention. Understanding SERP composition and optimizing for various elements is crucial for improving organic search performance and driving qualified traffic to websites.

Search Intent

The underlying goal or purpose behind a user's search query.

Key points:

- Also known as "user intent"

- Crucial for understanding and meeting user needs
- A significant factor in search engine ranking algorithms

Types of Search Intent:

1. Informational: Seeking knowledge or answers
2. Navigational: Looking for a specific website
3. Transactional: Ready to make a purchase or take action
4. Commercial Investigation: Researching products or services

Importance:

- Guides content creation and optimization
- Improves search engine rankings
- Enhances user satisfaction and engagement

Determining Search Intent:

- Analyze query language and modifiers
- Examine SERP features and top-ranking content
- Use keyword research tools to identify intent patterns

. . .

Optimization Strategies:

1. Align content with identified intent
2. Study competitor content for insights
3. Consider the “3 C’s”: Content type, format, and angle
4. Monitor SERP fluctuations for intent changes

Understanding and optimizing for search intent is crucial for effective SEO. It helps create content that satisfies user needs and aligns with search engine algorithms, leading to improved rankings and user engagement.

Search Term

The exact word or phrase that a user enters into a search engine to find information, products, or services.

Key points:

- Also known as search query
- Reflects user’s actual language and intent
- Distinct from keywords used by marketers

Importance for SEO:

- Reveals user intent and language preferences
- Guides keyword selection and content creation
- Influences search engine rankings

Characteristics:

- Can be short (1-2 words) or long-tail (3+ words)
- Often conversational or question-based
- May include misspellings or variations

Relation to Keywords:

- Search terms are user-generated
- Keywords are marketer-selected for targeting
- Keywords should align with common search terms

Analysis Methods:

1. Search term reports in Google Ads
2. Keyword research tools
3. Google Search Console data

Best Practices:

- Align content with common search terms
- Consider search intent behind terms
- Use long-tail variations for targeted content
- Regularly update based on trending search terms

UNDERSTANDING search terms is crucial for effective SEO and content strategy. It helps bridge the gap between user language and marketing terminology, leading to more relevant content and improved search visibility.

SEARCH VISIBILITY

The estimated percentage of clicks a website receives from its organic rankings for a set of keywords in search engine results.

KEY POINTS:

- Measures a site's prominence in organic search results
- Calculated as a percentage of total potential clicks
- Can be tracked for individual keywords or overall site performance

IMPORTANCE:

- Indicates SEO effectiveness

- Helps gauge market share in organic search
- Provides insights into ranking improvements or declines

Measurement:

- Use SEO tools like Ahrefs' Rank Tracker
- Calculate based on click estimates and ranking positions
- Track over time to observe trends

Improvement strategies:

1. Optimize for search intent
2. Build high-quality backlinks
3. Enhance internal linking structure
4. Create comprehensive, authoritative content
5. Improve technical SEO aspects

Considerations:

- 100% visibility is not achievable
- Varies by keyword and industry competitiveness
- Influenced by SERP features and paid ads

SEARCH VISIBILITY IS a crucial metric for understanding a website's performance in organic search results. It provides valuable insights for SEO strategy and helps measure the effectiveness of optimization efforts over time.

SEARCH VOLUME

The average number of times a specific keyword or search query is entered into a search engine over a given period, typically measured monthly.

KEY POINTS:

- Indicates keyword popularity and potential traffic
- Often based on annual averages
- May group similar keywords together

IMPORTANCE FOR SEO:

- Guides keyword selection and prioritization
- Helps estimate potential organic traffic
- Informs content strategy and planning

CONSIDERATIONS:

- Not always accurate or up-to-date
- Doesn't account for click-through rates

- Seasonal variations may affect accuracy

Best practices:

1. Consider Traffic Potential, not just search volume
2. Balance volume with keyword difficulty
3. Analyze search trends for context
4. Don't ignore low-volume, high-intent keywords

Measurement tools:

- Google Keyword Planner
- SEO tools like Ahrefs Keywords Explorer
- Google Trends for historical data

Limitations:

- Doesn't guarantee actual traffic
- May not reflect current search behavior
- Doesn't account for SERP features or paid ads

While search volume is a valuable metric for SEO and keyword research, it should be considered alongside other factors like keyword difficulty, search intent, and overall traffic potential for effective SEO strategy development.

. . .

Secondary Keywords

Related words and phrases that complement and support the primary keyword of a webpage or piece of content.

Key points:

- Include synonyms, subtopics, and long-tail variations
- Enhance topic coverage and content depth
- Improve search engine understanding of content

Importance:

- Expands potential keyword rankings
- Enhances content relevance and comprehensiveness
- Improves chances of ranking for multiple search queries

Finding secondary keywords:

1. Use content optimization tools
2. Analyze top-ranking pages' organic keywords
3. Utilize keyword research tools (e.g., Ahrefs Keywords Explorer)

. . .

Best practices:

- Incorporate naturally into content
- Use in subheadings and body text
- Balance with primary keyword focus
- Avoid keyword stuffing

SEO benefits:

- Increases organic search visibility
- Helps target long-tail search queries
- Supports topical authority

Secondary keywords play a crucial role in modern SEO strategy by expanding content relevance and improving search visibility. They help create comprehensive, user-focused content that can rank for a wide range of related search queries, enhancing overall SEO performance.

Secure Sockets Layer (SSL)

An internet security protocol designed to establish encrypted connections between web servers and clients.

Key points:

- Largely replaced by Transport Layer Security (TLS)
- Enables HTTPS for secure web browsing
- Protects data transmission and user privacy

Importance for SEO:

- HTTPS is a lightweight ranking factor
- Improves user trust and engagement
- Preserves referral data in analytics

Key components:

1. SSL/TLS certificates
2. Public and private key encryption
3. Certificate Authorities (CAs)

Types of certificates:

- Domain Validated (DV)
- Organization Validated (OV)
- Extended Validation (EV)

Best practices:

1. Obtain certificates from reputable CAs
2. Choose appropriate certificate type for needs
3. Renew certificates before expiration (max 398 days)

Considerations:

- Essential for e-commerce and data collection sites
- Impacts site speed when implemented with modern protocols
- Free options available for basic needs

SSL/TLS is crucial for website security and user trust. While the term SSL is still commonly used, modern implementations typically use TLS. Implementing HTTPS through SSL/TLS certificates is essential for SEO and overall website credibility.

Seed Keywords

Short, fundamental terms that serve as the starting point for keyword research and content strategy.

Key points:

- Usually one or two words long
- Represent core topics or products

- Used to generate more specific keyword ideas

Importance:

- Form the foundation of keyword research
- Help identify subtopics and topic clusters
- Guide overall content strategy

Characteristics:

- High search volume
- Often highly competitive
- Broad in nature

Finding Seed Keywords:

1. Brainstorm core business terms
2. Analyze competitor keywords
3. Check own website's ranking terms
4. Use Google's related searches and "People Also Ask" boxes
5. Explore industry forums and Q&A sites

Best practices:

- Start with multiple relevant seed keywords
- Use them to generate long-tail and related keywords
- Consider search intent behind each seed keyword
- Balance between broad and specific seed terms

CONSIDERATIONS:

- May be too competitive to target directly
- Serve as a starting point, not an end goal
- Should reflect core business offerings and user interests

SEED KEYWORDS ARE crucial for initiating comprehensive keyword research and developing a robust content strategy. They help SEO professionals and content creators explore a wide range of related terms and topics, enabling them to create content that aligns with user interests and search behaviors.

SEO (SEARCH ENGINE Optimization)

The practice of improving a website's visibility and ranking in organic search engine results.

KEY COMPONENTS:

1. Keyword Research: Identifying relevant search terms
2. On-Page SEO: Optimizing website content and structure
3. Off-Page SEO: Building backlinks and online reputation
4. Technical SEO: Enhancing website performance and crawlability
5. Local SEO: Optimizing for local search results

Importance:

- Drives free, organic traffic
- Builds credibility and authority
- Offers long-term, scalable results

Best practices:

- Create high-quality, relevant content
- Optimize for user experience and search intent
- Build natural, high-quality backlinks
- Ensure mobile-friendliness and fast page speed
- Use relevant schema markup

Considerations:

- Requires ongoing effort and adaptation

- Results may take time to materialize
- Must align with search engine guidelines

Learning SEO:

- Study fundamentals and stay updated on trends
- Practice on real websites
- Engage with SEO communities and resources

SEO is a crucial digital marketing strategy that helps websites improve their visibility in search results, driving targeted organic traffic. It involves a combination of technical, content, and promotional efforts to align with search engine algorithms and user needs.

SEO Audit

A comprehensive evaluation of a website's search engine optimization performance, identifying issues and opportunities for improvement.

Key components:

1. On-page SEO analysis
2. Off-page SEO assessment
3. Technical SEO review
4. Local SEO evaluation

. . .

IMPORTANCE:

- Identifies SEO weaknesses and strengths
- Uncovers optimization opportunities
- Helps maintain search engine compliance
- Guides SEO strategy development

FREQUENCY:

- Recommended every 3-6 months
- After significant website changes
- When experiencing sudden traffic drops

KEY AREAS OF FOCUS:

- Crawlability and indexability
- Content quality and relevance
- Backlink profile
- Site speed and mobile-friendliness
- Keyword optimization
- User experience factors

TOOLS FOR AUDITING:

- Google Search Console

- Ahrefs Site Audit
- PageSpeed Insights
- Other specialized SEO tools

Best practices:

- Use a comprehensive checklist
- Prioritize issues based on impact
- Implement changes systematically
- Monitor results post-audit

An SEO audit is a crucial process for maintaining and improving a website's search engine performance. It provides actionable insights for optimizing various aspects of a site, helping to enhance visibility, traffic, and overall online presence.

SEO Silo

A website architecture strategy that organizes content into distinct, topically-related groups to enhance search engine optimization.

Key points:

- Groups related pages into isolated categories
- Aims to improve topical relevance and authority
- Facilitates internal linking within topic clusters

. . .

Structure:

- Top-level category pages
- Subcategory pages
- Individual content pages

Proposed benefits:

- Enhances topical authority
- Improves internal link relevance
- Potentially boosts rankings for related keywords

Considerations:

- May limit cross-topic internal linking
- Can be overly rigid for some site structures
- Potential conflict with user-friendly navigation

Alternative approach:

- 'Pyramid' structure: more flexible internal linking
- Focus on user experience and natural topic relationships

. . .

Best practices:

- Organize content logically by topic
- Use relevant internal linking
- Prioritize user experience over strict silo adherence
- Balance SEO structure with intuitive navigation

While SEO silos can help organize content and potentially improve topical relevance, a more flexible approach focusing on natural topic relationships and user-friendly navigation is often preferred in modern SEO strategies.

SERP Features

Elements on search engine results pages (SERPs) that provide additional information or functionality beyond traditional organic listings.

Key points:

- Enhance user experience with rich, relevant content
- Can appear in various positions on SERPs
- May reduce clicks to organic listings

Common SERP Features:

1. Featured Snippets
2. People Also Ask
3. Knowledge Panels
4. Local Pack
5. Image Pack
6. Top Stories
7. Sitelinks
8. Shopping Results

Importance:

- Improve user experience and information accessibility
- Offer additional visibility opportunities for websites
- Can impact click-through rates of organic listings

Optimization strategies:

- Create concise, informative content for Featured Snippets
- Implement structured data for rich results
- Optimize images for Image Packs
- Focus on local SEO for Local Pack appearances

CONSIDERATIONS:

- Prevalence varies by query type and intent
- Can lead to zero-click searches
- Require specific optimization techniques

SERP FEATURES REPRESENT Google's efforts to provide more immediate, relevant answers to user queries. While they can offer increased visibility, they also present challenges for traditional SEO strategies by potentially reducing organic click-through rates.

SHARE OF VOICE (SOV)

A metric that measures a brand's visibility and presence in the market compared to its competitors. In SEO context:

- Represents a website's visibility in search results for specific keywords
- Indicates the proportion of clicks a site receives for target search queries

KEY ASPECTS:

1. Brand awareness measurement
2. Competitive benchmarking tool
3. Performance indicator across multiple channels

Importance:

- Assesses market position and growth potential
- Guides PR and marketing strategies
- Provides consumer and industry insights
- Helps track campaign effectiveness

Calculation:

SOV = Brand's metrics / Total market metrics

Measurement areas:

1. PPC (Impression Share)
2. Organic search visibility
3. Social media mentions
4. Media coverage

Improvement strategies:

- Create valuable, shareable content
- Increase social media engagement
- Establish thought leadership
- Optimize SEO practices

Tools for measurement:

- Google Ads (for PPC)
- Ahrefs Rank Tracker (for SEO)
- Social media analytics tools
- Media monitoring platforms

Share of Voice is a comprehensive metric for understanding a brand's overall market presence and effectiveness across various digital channels. It provides valuable insights for strategic decision-making in marketing and SEO efforts.

Short-Tail Keywords

Broad, high-volume search queries that typically cover general topics. Also known as "head terms."

Key points:

- Located at the "head" of the search demand curve
- Generally have high search volume (often >100k monthly searches)
- Not necessarily limited to one or two words

Characteristics:

- Broad in scope and meaning
- Highly competitive for SEO and PPC

- Often have lower conversion rates due to lack of specificity

Importance:

- Serve as "seed" keywords for broader keyword research
- Can drive significant traffic if ranked for
- Indicate overall market trends and interests

Challenges:

- Extremely competitive to rank for organically
- Often expensive in PPC campaigns
- May have lower click-through rates due to SERP features

Finding short-tail keywords:

1. Analyze Google Search Console data
2. Use SEO tools to research competitor keywords
3. Explore high-volume terms in keyword research tools

Considerations:

- Balance with long-tail and mid-tail keywords in strategy
- Evaluate actual traffic potential, not just search volume
- Consider user intent and conversion likelihood

SHORT-TAIL KEYWORDS ARE crucial for understanding broad market trends and initiating keyword research. While challenging to rank for, they can provide significant visibility and traffic when successfully targeted.

SITELINKS

Additional links displayed beneath a website's main search result, providing direct access to specific pages or sections of the site.

KEY POINTS:

- Generated automatically by Google
- Enhance SERP visibility and click-through rates
- Reflect site structure and perceived page importance

TYPES:

1. Organic sitelinks (standard): Multiple links below main result

2. Organic sitelinks (horizontal): Single row of links
3. Sitelink assets: Paid sitelinks in search ads

Importance:

- Increases SERP real estate
- Improves user navigation
- Potentially boosts organic traffic

Best practices for influencing sitelinks:

1. Use clear, informative titles and headings
2. Maintain logical site structure
3. Implement strong internal linking
4. Ensure content quality and relevance

Limitations:

- Cannot be directly edited or controlled
- Google determines which pages appear as sitelinks
- Removal options are limited (e.g., noindex tag)

Considerations:

- Appear for approximately 80% of searches
- More common for branded queries
- Reflect Google's understanding of site hierarchy

SITELINKS ARE a valuable SERP feature that can significantly enhance a website's visibility and user experience in search results. While not directly controllable, they can be influenced through good site structure and SEO practices.

SITEMAPS

An XML file that lists URLs on a website, providing information about content structure to search engines.

KEY POINTS:

- Helps search engines discover and index website pages
- Can include additional data like last modification dates
- Not mandatory but highly recommended for SEO

IMPORTANCE:

- Facilitates faster page discovery
- Provides a complete view of website structure
- Signals page importance to search engines

. . .

Best practices:

1. Create comprehensive sitemaps
2. Ensure important pages aren't excluded
3. Submit sitemaps to search engines
4. Keep sitemaps updated

Types:

- XML sitemaps (most common)
- RSS/Atom feeds
- Text file sitemaps

Submission:

- Google Search Console for Google
- Bing Webmaster Tools for Bing
- Can be referenced in robots.txt file

Considerations:

- Exclude noindexed and low-value pages
- Limit to 50,000 URLs or 50MB per sitemap file
- Use sitemap index files for larger sites

. . .

Sitemaps are a crucial tool for effective SEO, helping to ensure that search engines can find and index all important pages on a website. While not a ranking factor itself, sitemaps contribute to better crawling and indexing, which can indirectly impact search visibility.

Sitewide Link

A hyperlink that appears on every page of a website, typically in the header, footer, or navigation menu.

Key points:

- Can be internal (linking to other pages on the same site) or external (linking to other websites)
- Common examples include links to privacy policies, terms of service, or social media profiles

In backlink context:

- Refers to a link from another website that appears on all of its pages
- Often considered unnatural and may violate search engine guidelines

Importance:

- Provides easy access to important pages or information
- Can pass significant link equity if external
- May be seen as manipulative if used excessively for SEO purposes

Considerations:

- Overuse of external sitewide links can be flagged as spam
- Internal sitewide links help with site navigation and structure
- Search engines may devalue or ignore excessive sitewide links

Best practices:

- Use sitewide links judiciously and naturally
- Ensure relevance and value to users
- Avoid sitewide linking schemes for SEO purposes

While sitewide links can be legitimate for navigation and user experience, in the context of SEO and link building, they should be used cautiously to avoid potential penalties from search engines.

. . .

Spamdexing

The practice of manipulating search engine algorithms to artificially improve a website's rankings, violating search engine guidelines. Also known as webspam or black-hat SEO.

Key points:

- Aims to deceive search engines and users
- Provides no value to searchers
- Actively combated by search engines (e.g., Google's SpamBrain)

Common techniques:

1. Content spam:

- Automatically generated content
- Cloaking
- Hidden text
- Keyword stuffing
- Scraped content

2. Link spam:

- Private Blog Networks (PBNs)
- Paid links
- Excessive link exchanges
- Link injection

. . .

Risks:

- Search engine penalties
- De-indexing of website
- Loss of organic traffic and rankings

Best practice:

- Avoid all spamdexing techniques
- Focus on creating valuable, user-focused content
- Use white-hat SEO strategies for sustainable growth

While some spamdexing techniques may provide short-term gains in certain industries, they are highly risky and unsustainable for long-term SEO success. Search engines continually improve their ability to detect and penalize such practices.

Sponsored Link Attribute

An HTML attribute (rel="sponsored") used to indicate links that are part of advertisements, paid placements, or sponsorships.

Key points:

- Introduced by Google in 2019
- Part of evolving link attribution system
- Applies to paid links, sponsored content, and affiliate links

USAGE:

Sponsored link

IMPORTANCE:

- Helps search engines understand link context
- Supports transparency in link relationships
- Part of Google's efforts to combat link spam

RELATION TO OTHER ATTRIBUTES:

- Can replace rel="nofollow" for paid links
- Used alongside rel="ugc" for user-generated content
- Multiple attributes can be applied to a single link

SEO IMPLICATIONS:

- Treated as a "hint" by Google, not a directive
- May or may not prevent passing of link equity

- Does not guarantee immunity from link scheme penalties

Best practices:

- Use for all paid or sponsored links
- Apply to affiliate links when possible
- Can be used in combination with other rel attributes

While not mandatory, using the sponsored link attribute is recommended for transparency and adherence to search engine guidelines. It helps maintain a clear distinction between organic and paid links on a website.

Structured Data

A standardized format for providing additional, machine-readable information about web page content to search engines and other applications.

Key points:

- Uses schema.org vocabulary
- Enhances search engine understanding of content
- Enables rich results in search engine results pages (SERPs)

. . .

IMPLEMENTATION FORMATS:

1. JSON-LD (most common and recommended)
2. Microdata
3. RDFa

COMMON TYPES:

- Article
- Product
- Event
- Review
- Local Business
- Recipe

IMPORTANCE:

- Improves content visibility in search results
- Enables rich snippets and other SERP features
- Enhances user experience with more informative search listings

BENEFITS:

- Potentially higher click-through rates

- Better content categorization by search engines
- Improved chances for featured snippets

IMPLEMENTATION BEST PRACTICES:

- Use Google's supported schema types
- Implement JSON-LD when possible
- Test using Google's Rich Results Test tool
- Keep structured data consistent with visible content

CONSIDERATIONS:

- Not all schema types are supported by all search engines
- Implementation doesn't guarantee rich results
- Should accurately represent page content

STRUCTURED DATA IS a powerful tool for enhancing how search engines interpret and display web content. It plays a crucial role in modern SEO by enabling more informative and visually appealing search results.

SUBDOMAIN

A division of a website's domain that creates a separate section or subsection of the main site.

. . .

Key points:

- Structure: [subdomain].domain.com
- Example: blog.example.com

Characteristics:

- Part of the main domain but can function independently
- Can have its own content management system or platform
- Allows for organization of large websites

SEO implications:

- No inherent SEO advantage over subfolders
- Treated similarly to subfolders by Google
- May take slightly longer for Google to understand site structure

Benefits:

- Organizational flexibility
- Separate hosting and management possible
- Useful for international targeting

- Simplifies complex URL structures

CONSIDERATIONS:

- Requires separate SSL certificates (unless using wildcard)
- Needs its own robots.txt file
- May need separate Google Search Console property

BEST PRACTICES:

1. Interlink with main domain
2. Ensure consistent branding and user experience
3. Implement proper tracking across all subdomains
4. Use hreflang tags for international versions

SUBDOMAINS OFFER a way to organize and structure large websites or separate distinct sections of a site. While they don't provide SEO advantages over subfolders, they can be beneficial for site organization and management in certain scenarios.

TAXONOMY SEO

The practice of organizing and categorizing website

content in a structured, hierarchical manner to improve both user experience and search engine understanding.

Key points:

- Involves creating logical content categories and subcategories
- Includes elements like tags, categories, and hierarchical structures
- Enhances site navigation and content discoverability

Importance:

- Improves user experience and site navigation
- Helps search engines understand site structure and content relationships
- Supports better internal linking strategies

Components:

1. Categories: Broad groupings of content
2. Subcategories: More specific content groupings within categories
3. Tags: Cross-sectional content labels

SEO benefits:

- Enhances crawlability and indexability
- Supports topical relevance and authority
- Improves internal link structure

Best practices:

1. Create a logical, intuitive hierarchy
2. Use clear, descriptive category and tag names
3. Avoid excessive categories or tags
4. Implement consistent URL structures
5. Optimize category and tag pages for search

Considerations:

- Balance between depth and breadth of categories
- Regularly review and update taxonomy structure
- Align taxonomy with user search behavior and intent

Taxonomy SEO is crucial for organizing large amounts of content effectively, improving both user navigation and search engine understanding of a website's structure and topical focus.

. . .

Technical SEO

The practice of optimizing a website's technical elements to improve its crawling, indexing, and rendering by search engines. Key components:

1. Site structure and architecture
2. Crawlability and indexability
3. Website performance and speed
4. Mobile-friendliness
5. Security (HTTPS)
6. Structured data implementation

Importance:

- Ensures search engines can access and understand content
- Improves overall website performance and user experience
- Supports better search engine rankings

Key areas of focus:

- XML sitemaps
- Robots.txt file
- URL structure
- Page load speed
- Core Web Vitals
- Canonical tags

- Hreflang tags
- Schema markup

Best practices:

1. Conduct regular technical SEO audits
2. Implement HTTPS across the site
3. Optimize for mobile-first indexing
4. Improve page load speeds
5. Use structured data where appropriate
6. Ensure proper crawl budget management

Tools:

- Google Search Console
- Ahrefs Site Audit
- PageSpeed Insights
- Mobile-Friendly Test

Technical SEO forms the foundation of a website's search engine optimization efforts. By ensuring that a site is technically sound, it creates the basis for other SEO efforts to be more effective, ultimately leading to better visibility and performance in search results.

Thin Content

Web pages with little or no original, valuable content that fail to meet user needs or search engine quality standards.

Key points:

- Often targeted by search engine algorithms (e.g., Google Panda)
- Can lead to manual penalties from search engines
- Not necessarily related to word count

Types of thin content:

1. Automatically generated content
2. Thin affiliate pages
3. Scraped content
4. Doorway pages
5. Low-value or duplicate content

SEO implications:

- Negatively impacts search rankings
- Can lead to site-wide penalties
- Reduces overall site quality in search engines' view

Identification:

- Low engagement metrics (high bounce rates, low time on page)
- Lack of organic traffic
- Poor user feedback or reviews

Best practices to avoid:

1. Create original, high-quality content
2. Focus on user value and intent
3. Regularly audit and improve existing content
4. Consolidate or remove low-value pages
5. Ensure affiliate content adds unique value

Considerations:

- Quality over quantity in content creation
- Importance of meeting user needs and expectations
- Role of content in building site authority and trust

Thin content is a significant concern in SEO, as it can severely impact a website's search performance and user experience. Focusing on creating valuable, original content is crucial for avoiding thin content issues and maintaining strong search visibility.

Tiered Link Building

A link building strategy that creates multiple layers of backlinks to boost the authority of primary links pointing to a target website.

Key points:

- Considered a grey or black-hat SEO technique
- Violates Google's webmaster guidelines
- Structured in a pyramid-like hierarchy

Structure:

1. Tier 1: Direct, high-quality links to target site
2. Tier 2: Links pointing to Tier 1 pages
3. Tier 3 (optional): Links pointing to Tier 2 pages

Purpose:

- Enhance authority of primary backlinks
- Improve search engine rankings indirectly
- Distribute link equity across multiple levels

Risks:

- Potential for search engine penalties
- Decreased link quality in lower tiers
- Difficulty in maintaining natural link profiles

Considerations:

- Not recommended for sustainable SEO strategies
- Requires significant time and resource investment
- Can be detected and devalued by search engines

Alternatives:

- Focus on earning high-quality, natural backlinks
- Develop valuable, shareable content
- Engage in legitimate outreach and relationship building

While tiered link building aims to amplify the impact of backlinks, it's considered manipulative and risky. Modern SEO practices favor earning natural, high-quality backlinks through valuable content and legitimate relationships.

Title Tag

An HTML element that specifies the title of a web page.

Key points:

- HTML syntax: Page Title
- Appears in search engine results pages (SERPs)
- Displays in browser tabs and social media shares

Importance:

- Crucial for SEO and click-through rates
- Influences user's first impression of page content
- Used by search engines to understand page topic

Best practices:

1. Include primary keyword
2. Keep length under 50-60 characters
3. Make each title unique and engaging
4. Accurately represent page content

SEO considerations:

- Major factor in search engine rankings
- Impacts click-through rates from SERPs
- Google may rewrite titles for search results

. . .

Display variations:

- SERPs: May be truncated or rewritten by Google
- Browser tabs: Often shortened
- Social media: Used for link previews

Tips:

- Use title tag preview tools for optimal length
- Can differ from H1 tag on page
- Avoid keyword stuffing
- Focus on clarity and relevance

The title tag is a critical element for both SEO and user experience. It serves as a concise summary of page content, influencing how search engines interpret the page and how users decide whether to click through to the site.

Top-Level Domain (TLD)

The last segment of a domain name, following the final dot.

Key points:

- Highest level in the Domain Name System (DNS) hierarchy
- Managed by organizations under ICANN oversight

Types:

1. Generic (gTLD): e.g., .com, .org, .net
2. Country Code (ccTLD): e.g., .uk, .de, .jp
3. Sponsored (sTLD): e.g., .edu, .gov
4. Infrastructure: .arpa

SEO Importance:

- Can influence local search rankings (ccTLDs)
- Some TLDs associated with spam may affect trust
- Keywords in TLDs don't directly improve rankings

Best Practices:

1. Prefer .com, .org, or .net for general use
2. Use ccTLDs for country-specific targeting
3. Be cautious with non-standard TLDs

Considerations:

- ccTLDs strongly signal geographic targeting
- Some ccTLDs (e.g., .io) treated as gTLDs by Google
- New gTLDs offer creative branding opportunities

TLDs play a role in branding, user trust, and sometimes in search engine interpretation of a website's target audience. While not a direct ranking factor, choosing the right TLD can impact a site's overall SEO strategy and performance in specific markets.

Topical Relevance

The degree to which a webpage's content aligns with a specific subject or theme, moving beyond simple keyword matching.

Key points:

- Focuses on comprehensive topic coverage
- Applies to both on-page content and link building
- Emphasizes contextual relationships between topics

Importance for SEO:

- Enhances content quality and depth
- Improves search engine understanding of content
- Potentially boosts search rankings

Key aspects:

1. In-depth subject coverage
2. Addressing related subtopics
3. Answering user questions within the topic
4. Contextual linking to related content

Benefits:

- Improved user experience
- Increased perceived authority on a topic
- Better alignment with search intent

Implementation strategies:

1. Create comprehensive, topic-focused content
2. Develop content clusters around main themes
3. Use internal linking to connect related topics
4. Acquire backlinks from topically relevant sources

Considerations:

- Balance between depth and breadth of coverage
- Evolving with user search behaviors and interests
- Aligning with overall content strategy

Topical relevance is crucial in modern SEO, reflecting a shift towards more meaningful, context-driven content creation and link building. It helps establish expertise and authority in specific subject areas, potentially leading to improved search visibility and user engagement.

Transport Layer Security (TLS)

A cryptographic protocol that provides secure communication over the internet.

Key points:

- Successor to Secure Sockets Layer (SSL)
- Essential component of HTTPS
- Ensures privacy and data integrity

Function:

- Encrypts data transmitted between client and server
- Authenticates communicating parties

- Prevents eavesdropping and data tampering

Importance for SEO:

- Google uses HTTPS as a ranking signal
- Improves user trust and site credibility
- Essential for e-commerce and data collection sites

Implementation:

- Requires TLS certificate from a Certificate Authority (CA)
- Applied at the server level
- Indicated by padlock icon in browser address bar

Versions:

- TLS 1.2 and 1.3 are current standards
- Older versions (TLS 1.0, 1.1) are deprecated

Best practices:

- Use the latest TLS version
- Regularly update and renew certificates

- Implement across entire website, not just login pages

CONSIDERATIONS:

- Minor impact on page load speed
- Necessary for compliance with data protection regulations
- Supports other security features like HSTS

TLS IS crucial for website security and user privacy. Its implementation is considered standard practice in modern web development and is essential for maintaining trust with users and search engines alike.

UGC Link Attribute

An HTML attribute (rel="ugc") that indicates to search engines that a link appears in user-generated content.

KEY POINTS:

- Introduced by Google in 2019
- Applies to comments, forum posts, and other user-submitted content
- Helps search engines understand link context and origin

SEO implications:

- Minimal direct impact on rankings
- Recommended for links in user-submitted content
- Helps prevent potential penalties for unnatural external links

Usage:

- Less than 1% of websites currently utilize this attribute
- Can be combined with "nofollow" attribute
- Alternatives include using only "nofollow" for user-generated links

The UGC attribute provides additional context to search engines about link sources, potentially improving overall site quality signals and reducing spam concerns.

Unnatural Links

Artificially created backlinks designed to manipulate search engine rankings, violating search engine guidelines.

Key characteristics:

* Not editorially placed or vouched for by site owners

* Often involve paid links, link exchanges, or automated link creation

* Can include over-optimized anchor texts or low-quality directory listings

. . .

SEO implications:

* Short-term ranking boosts possible
* High risk of penalties and dramatic ranking drops
* Difficult to recover from penalties

Detection methods:

1. Excessive links from single domains
2. Numerous links from low-authority sites
3. Unnatural patterns in anchor text usage
4. Poor quality of referring websites

Best practices:

* Regularly audit backlink profiles
* Use white-hat link building strategies
* Consider disavowing suspicious links
* Exercise caution when outsourcing SEO services

While potentially effective short-term, unnatural links pose significant risks to long-term SEO success and should be avoided in favor of legitimate link-building strategies.

URL Rating (UR)

An Ahrefs metric measuring the strength of a webpage's backlink profile on a scale of 0 to 100.

Key features:

* Logarithmic scale (100 being strongest)
* Considers both internal and external backlinks
* Only "dofollow" links contribute to UR

SEO IMPLICATIONS:

* Positive correlation with Google rankings
* Helps assess individual page strength
* Distinct from Domain Rating (DR)

CHARACTERISTICS:

* Page-level metric
* Similar concept to Google's PageRank
* Influenced by quantity and quality of backlinks

URL RATING PROVIDES insight into a specific page's link authority, offering a useful indicator of its potential to rank well in search results. It's a valuable tool for comparing page strength and identifying high-performing content within a website or across competitors.

URL Slug

The part of a URL following the domain name or subfolder, typically describing the page's content.

KEY CHARACTERISTICS:

* Follows the "/" after domain or subfolder
* Excludes URL parameters and hash parameters
* Often readable and descriptive

. . .

SEO IMPLICATIONS:

* Lightweight ranking factor
* More important for user experience than SEO
* Helps search engines understand content pre-indexing

BEST PRACTICES:

1. Keep short but informative
2. Use hyphens to separate words
3. Avoid dates in slugs
4. Use lowercase letters

IMPORTANCE:

* Improves user understanding of page content
* Increases click-through likelihood
* Enhances memorability and shareability

WHILE NOT A MAJOR RANKING FACTOR, well-crafted URL slugs contribute to overall user experience and can indirectly benefit SEO by encouraging clicks and shares. They should be designed primarily for user clarity rather than keyword optimization.

USER INTENT

The underlying purpose or goal behind a user's search query.

. . .

Key aspects:

* Also known as search intent
* Reflects what users truly seek when searching
* Crucial for effective SEO and content creation

Types of intent:

1. Informational: Seeking knowledge or answers
2. Navigational: Looking for a specific website
3. Transactional: Intending to make a purchase
4. Commercial investigation: Researching products or services

SEO implications:

* Guides content creation strategy
* Influences keyword targeting
* Affects SERP features and rankings

Importance:

* Aligns content with user expectations
* Improves user satisfaction and engagement
* Potentially boosts search engine rankings

Understanding user intent helps create more relevant, targeted content that satisfies searchers' needs, potentially leading to improved search performance and user experience.

Vertical Search

A specialized search engine focusing on a specific industry, content type, or segment of the overall search landscape.

Key characteristics:

* Also known as specialty or topical search
* Searches within a limited, specific data set
* Provides more targeted results than general search engines

Examples:

* E-commerce: Amazon, eBay
* Travel: Airbnb, Skyscanner
* Employment: Indeed, Glassdoor
* Local: Yelp

Importance:

* Delivers more relevant results for niche topics
* Reduces information overload for users
* Offers businesses access to targeted audiences

Comparison to horizontal search:

* Vertical: Focused on specific topics or content types
* Horizontal: Covers entire web (e.g., Google's main search)

. . .

SEO IMPLICATIONS:

* Requires Vertical Search Optimization (VSO)
* Provides less competitive path to targeted audiences
* Can complement traditional SEO strategies

VERTICAL SEARCH ENGINES cater to specific user needs, offering more focused results than general search engines. They present opportunities for businesses to reach highly targeted audiences and for users to find relevant information more efficiently.

WEBSITE AUTHORITY

A concept in SEO representing a domain's overall strength and likelihood to rank well in search results.

Key aspects:

- Not an official Google ranking factor
- Often measured by third-party metrics (e.g., Domain Rating, Domain Authority)
- Primarily influenced by backlink profile quality and quantity

Importance for SEO:

- Correlates with organic keyword rankings
- Aids in comparing website strength within a niche
- Helps evaluate potential link-building opportunities

Factors affecting authority:

- Quality and relevance of backlinks
- Content quality and relevance
- Technical SEO elements (e.g., site speed, mobile-friendliness)

Best practices:

1. Focus on creating high-quality, relevant content
2. Earn diverse, high-quality backlinks
3. Don't ignore lower-authority but relevant sites for backlinks
4. Avoid artificial inflation of authority metrics

While not a direct ranking factor, website authority serves as a useful indicator of a site's potential to perform well in search results. It should be considered alongside other SEO metrics for a comprehensive understanding of a site's strength.

Website Hit

A server request for any element of a webpage, including HTML files, images, stylesheets, and scripts.

Key characteristics:

- Counts each file request separately
- Often misinterpreted as equivalent to pageviews
- Can be misleading as a measure of website traffic

Distinctions:

- Hit: Any server request for a file
- Pageview: Loading of a single webpage
- Unique Visitor: Individual user visiting the site
- Session: Set of user interactions within a timeframe

SEO implications:

- Not a reliable metric for measuring site performance
- Can inflate perceived traffic numbers
- Less relevant than pageviews, unique visitors, or sessions

Importance:

- Understanding the difference aids in accurate traffic analysis
- Helps avoid misinterpretation of website analytics
- Encourages focus on more meaningful engagement metrics

While website hits provide server-level data, they offer limited insight into actual user engagement or site performance. SEO professionals should prioritize more user-centric metrics for meaningful analysis and strategy development.

Website Structure

The organizational framework of a website's pages and their interconnections.

Key aspects:

- Also known as website architecture
- Determines navigation paths for users and search crawlers
- Often follows a hierarchical "pyramid" model

Importance for UX:

- Facilitates intuitive navigation
- Improves information findability
- Enhances overall user experience

SEO implications:

- Aids search engine crawling and indexing
- Helps distribute link equity across pages
- Indicates page priority through internal linking

Best practices:

1. Use clear, logical hierarchies
2. Implement effective internal linking
3. Create a user-friendly navigation menu
4. Utilize breadcrumbs for complex sites
5. Maintain a shallow click depth (3-4 clicks max to any page)

Benefits:

- Increased time on site and return rate
- Improved search engine visibility
- Enhanced content discoverability

A well-planned website structure forms the foundation for both positive user experiences and effective SEO. It guides visitors and search engines through your content, potentially improving engagement metrics and search rankings.

White-hat SEO

Ethical search engine optimization practices that adhere to search engine guidelines and prioritize user experience.

Key characteristics:

- Focuses on long-term, sustainable results
- Prioritizes user experience over quick gains
- Follows search engine guidelines

Best practices:

1. Focus on a single, high-quality website
2. Create unique, valuable content (10x content approach)
3. Build natural, high-quality backlinks
4. Satisfy user search intent
5. Improve site structure and technical SEO

Importance:

- Builds sustainable organic traffic growth
- Minimizes risk of penalties from search engines
- Enhances overall user experience and brand reputation

Comparison:

- White-hat: Ethical, long-term approach
- Black-hat: Manipulative, high-risk tactics
- Grey-hat: Combination of white and black-hat techniques

Challenges:

- May take longer to see results
- Requires consistent effort and quality content production
- Competitive in high-value niches

Key points:

- Primarily based on the quality and quantity of a site's backlink profile
- Often measured by third-party metrics like Domain Authority (Moz) or Domain Rating (Ahrefs)
- Not solely determinative of rankings; content quality and relevance remain crucial
- Built through acquiring high-quality, relevant backlinks and creating valuable content
- Should be viewed as a long-term strategy, not a quick fix for SEO performance

White-hat SEO focuses on creating value for users while adhering to search engine guidelines. While it may require more time and effort, it provides a stable foundation for long-term organic search success and protects against potential penalties.

AFTERWORD

The AI revolution in SEO offers exciting opportunities for businesses and individuals to enhance their online presence. By understanding and leveraging these technologies, you're well-positioned to thrive in the digital future.

Remember, the goal of SEO remains the same: to connect valuable content with the people who are searching for it. AI is a powerful tool to help achieve this goal more effectively and efficiently than ever before.

As you close this book, I hope you feel empowered and excited about the possibilities that AI brings to SEO. The future of digital marketing is here, and it's more accessible than you might have thought. Embrace it, experiment with it, and use it to take your online presence to new heights.

Thank you for joining me on this journey through the world of AI and SEO. Here's to your success in the AI-powered digital landscape!

ABOUT THE AUTHOR

Andrew is a seasoned Lead Senior Software Engineer with over two decades of experience in the tech industry. Born in Poland, his original name is Andrzej. After moving to the USA, he adopted the name Andrew and currently uses both names.

He discovered his passion for programming at the tender age of 10 when he wrote his first program on an 8-bit ZX Spectrum computer. This early fascination with technology set the stage for a lifelong journey in the world of coding and artificial intelligence.

Andrzej's academic journey led him to the Military University of Technology in Warsaw, where he earned both an Engineering Degree in Cybernetics and a Master's Degree in Computer Science, specializing in Artificial Intelligence. This solid educational foundation, combined with his natural curiosity and drive, has enabled him to stay at the forefront of technological advancements throughout his career.

With expertise spanning various programming languages and frameworks, including JavaScript, PHP, Laravel, Svelte, and React, Andrzej has consistently pushed the boundaries of what's possible in web and mobile application development. His experience in the luxury yacht industry, where he spent nearly a decade creating innovative solutions, has given him unique insights into applying cutting-edge technology to niche markets.

Andrzej's passion for AI and its practical applications in SEO and content creation led him to write this book. Drawing from his vast experience and continuous learning in the field, he aims to bridge the gap between complex AI concepts and their real-world implementation in digital marketing and content strategies.

When he's not coding or exploring new AI technologies, Andrzej enjoys traveling and experiencing different cultures. His move from Poland to sunny Florida in 2015 reflects his adventurous spirit and adaptability – qualities that also shine through in his approach to technology and problem-solving.

Through this book, Andrzej shares his expertise and passion, hoping to inspire and guide others in leveraging the power of AI for SEO and content creation. His practical, hands-on approach makes complex topics accessible, reflecting his belief that with the right tools and knowledge, anyone can harness the potential of AI to revolutionize their digital strategies.

Andrzej is pursuing his Ph.D. in Artificial Intelligence, further deepening his expertise in this rapidly evolving field. His doctoral research focuses on advanced applications of AI in digital marketing and content creation, perfectly aligning with the themes explored in this book. This ongoing academic pursuit not only enriches Andrzej's understanding of AI's cutting-edge developments but also allows him to bridge the gap between theoretical advancements and practical industry applications. Through his doctoral work, Andrzej continues to push the boundaries of what's possible in AI-driven SEO and content strategies, bringing fresh insights and innovative approaches to the readers of this book.

https://andrewbus.com

https://x.com/AndrewPaulBus